D0173518

PALMETTO JOURNAL

ALSO BY PHILLIP MANNING

Afoot in the South: Walks in the Natural Areas of North Carolina

PALMETTO JOURNAL
Walks in the Natural Areas of South Carolina

PHILLIP MANNING
Illustrations by Diane Manning

JOHN F. BLAIR, PUBLISHER WINSTON-SALEM, NORTH CAROLINA

Copyright © 1995 by Phillip Manning
Printed in the United States of America
All Rights Reserved

DESIGN BY DEBRA LONG HAMPTON
MAPS AND COMPOSITION BY LIZA LANGRALL
ILLUSTRATIONS BY DIANE MANNING
PRINTED AND BOUND BY R. R. DONNELLEY & SONS

The paper in this book meets the guidelines for permanence and durability of the Committee on Production Guidelines for Book Longevity of the Council on Library Resources.

Library of Congress Cataloging-in-Publication Data
Manning, Phillip, 1936–
Palmetto journal : walks in the natural areas of South Carolina / Phillip Manning.
p. cm.
Includes index.
ISBN 0-89587-124-6
1. Natural history—South Carolina—Guidebooks. 2. Natural areas—South Carolina—Guidebooks. 3. Walking—South Carolina—Guidebooks. 4. Hiking—South Carolina—Guidebooks. 5. South Carolina—Guidebooks. I. Title.
QH105.S6M36 1995
508.757—dc20 94–49584

For
Eileen Benson Manning Elliott
(1914–1986)
who taught me about the state—and more.

It is inconceivable to me that
we can adjust ourselves to the
complexities of the land mechanism
without an intense curiosity to
understand its workings and an
habitual personal study of those
workings. The urge to comprehend
must precede the urge to reform.

Aldo Leopold, *Round River*

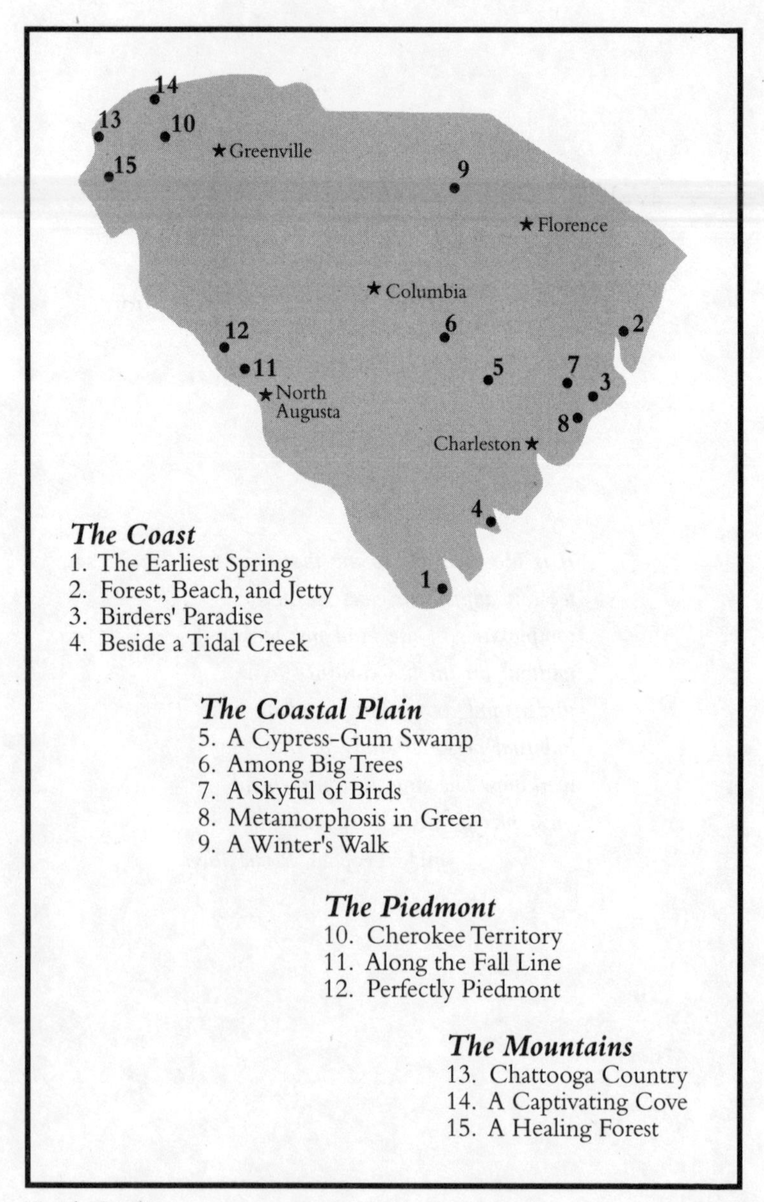

South Carolina

Contents

THE PIEDMONT

THE MOUNTAINS

Introduction

Biophilia is a new theory proposed by E.O. Wilson of Harvard University, one of the world's top evolutionary biologists. It posits that we humans are genetically attracted to natural areas because of how and where our species evolved. The theory has not been thoroughly investigated and is, perhaps, unprovable. But I think the idea has merit, and it certainly offers a handy rationale for a choice I made.

"Yes, dear, I have quit my job so I can spend more time in the woods. It's a genetic thing. We call it biophilia."

Walking in natural areas is a great delight for me. Diane, my wife and the illustrator of this book, loves the outdoors, too. We have been wandering through parks and forests and wildlife refuges for years, and she went along on most of the walks in this book. Because I grew up in South Carolina and worked there as a young man, my file folders bulge with material that I picked up twenty-five or more years ago, when I first walked many of these trails. On my desk, for example, is a 1968 brochure from Carolina Sandhills National Wildlife Refuge; a 1976 advertisement for a trout fishing seminar at Oconee State Park; some notes about a canoe trip in Congaree swamp, long before it became Congaree Swamp National Monument; and so forth. But no matter how many times I have been to a place, a new visit always teaches me something I didn't know. Natural areas are complicated, ever-changing places. They remind me of the old joke about Columbia (and a lot of other cities): it will be a nice town—if they ever finish it.

Like towns, natural areas are never finished. The landscape at Francis Marion National Forest barely resembles the one that existed there six years ago before Hurricane Hugo. And the pre-Hugo forest of the twentieth century was different from the one that covered that land in Francis Marion's time. The longleaf pine and wire grass that the Swamp Fox knew were cleared by settlers, and loblolly pines and oaks marched across the land after it was abandoned. These, in turn, were mostly destroyed by the storm and are now being replaced by . . . longleaf pines.

Despite superficial changes, though, I believe the land has a soul, an irreducible essence, and that a part of every natural landscape is timeless, or nearly so. Over 250 years ago, John Lawson, an early surveyor and explorer of the Carolinas, described a Piedmont forest that closely resembles one that stands today in the Long Cane Scenic Area of Sumter National Forest—in spite of logging and abuse. Even in Hugo-altered Francis Marion National Forest, wisps of pre-European flora and fauna persist. Charles Cotesworth Pinckney would likely recognize Pinckney Island today, even though the cotton fields he planted there after the Revolutionary War have long since vanished. It is, in fact, this mixture of constance and change, the way cultural and natural history mingle to shape the land, that makes the natural areas of South Carolina so intriguing and so worth a visit.

When I go to a natural area, I ask myself two questions: what is the land like, and how did it get that way? The rest of the day or weekend or week is spent searching for answers. That means I have to look around. And, for me, the only satisfactory way to look around—to really see a place—is to walk the trails, to get out into the woods or on the beach or in the marsh. After the field work is complete, I talk to anybody that knows something about the place and read everything I can get my hands on. Even so, I know my answers are incomplete, that there's always more to learn, so I also try to just enjoy myself. This, it turns out, is probably the best reason to visit South Carolina's natural areas: to see its marshes and old rice fields, its rolling hills and surprisingly rugged mountains; to watch perky Carolina wrens and elegant swallow-tailed kites; to spy on alligators and beavers, bald-faced hornets and red-spotted newts. And if all that is not enough of a reason, if you need to further explain your hunger to go into natural areas—either to yourself or to someone else—you might want to trot out biophilia. It's only a theory, but it's a useful theory.

South Carolina is a naturalist's delight. It rises from sea level along the Atlantic coast to 3,554 feet at its highest point, Sassafras Mountain, a peak in the Appalachian range. According to a South Carolina Wildlife and Marine Resources bulletin written by John B. Nelson, the state has sixty-seven different natural communities, ranging from "Acidic Cliff" to "Xeric Sandhill Scrub." Much of this diversity arises from the state's geography. South Carolina is divided into three physiographic provinces—the coastal plains, the Piedmont, and the mountains. Because this book is organized from a naturalist's point of view, I have subdivided the coastal plains into two regions, treating the coast as a separate province. This is not geologically correct, but I believe the natural communities found at the coast differ enough from those of the inner coastal plains to justify separating them.

Within each of the four provinces, I have selected several walks—none of which requires backpacking—to illustrate the natural habitats of that province. The windswept sprawl of marshes and impoundments at Santee Coastal Reserve is an example of one habitat of the coastal plains, while the beautiful hardwood coves near Caesars Head State Park are an example of a habitat found in the mountains.

As in the previous book in this series, each chapter is composed of three parts and concerns itself with one walk. The first part consists of a map, directions to trailhead, a brief description of the route, the length of the walk, and its degree of difficulty (from "easy" to "moderate" to "strenuous"). The second part describes the walk and the land through which it passes. It also tells of historical events that affected the land and made it what it is today. The third section of each chapter gives the hard information that readers would need to take the walk themselves—who to write or call, where to stay, any special precautions that may exist, and a bibliography.

Many of the trails in this book have been around awhile, and I hope that fifty or even a hundred years from now, a hiker will be able to walk to the ancient midden that is the terminus of the Indian Mound Trail in Edisto Beach State Park. I hope our grandsons and granddaughters can still take the Oak Ridge Trail into the back country of Congaree Swamp National Monument and wander among the towering trees there. And I hope that the Chattooga River and the great forests along its banks will remain safe from the axe wielders and dam builders.

For these things to be so, we must be vigilant. Every one of these walks is on publicly owned land—our land. And we must pay the same attention to it that we do to our own property. We must attend hearings that concern it; we must write letters about it; and we must fight for it. If we don't, our natural communities will slip away from us as surely as the gray wolf has vanished from the mountains and the Carolina parakeet from the coastal plains.

Most of these walks are on trails that are safer than the sidewalks of most cities. But you can still get lost or develop a blister or get caught in a storm. At one time or another, you will almost certainly be bitten by mosquitoes or ticks or no-see-ums. So, even though natural areas are not unusually dangerous places, it does make sense to take a few precautions.

If I walk alone, I always let someone know where I am going and when I expect to be back. I also take a few safety-related items in my pack when I spend a day in the field:

- Map
- Compass
- Band-Aids
- Pocket knife
- DEET (or some other insect repellent)
- Skin-So-Soft (for no-see-ums)
- Full water bottle
- Matches
- Lightweight, waterproof windbreaker
- Clean, dry bandanna or handkerchief
- Aspirin or ibuprofen

This the same list I included in the first book, and aside from the water, it all still weighs only a pound or two and still costs less than a hundred dollars.

THE COAST

The Countrey abounds with Grapes, large Figs, and Peaches; the woods with Deer, Conies, Turkeys, Quails, Curlues, Plovers, Teile, Herons; and, as the Indians say, in winter with Swans, Geese, Cranes, Duck and Mallard, and innumerable of other water-Fouls, whose names we know not. . . .

William Hilton, 1664

White Point Trail
Pinckney Island National Wildlife Refuge

From I-95, take U.S. 278 east toward Hilton Head.
After crossing the bridge over Mackay Creek, a signed exit leads
to a parking lot for the 4,053-acre refuge and the trailhead.
From the trailhead, walk north on the
well-maintained dirt road that leads to White Point.
Return by the same route.

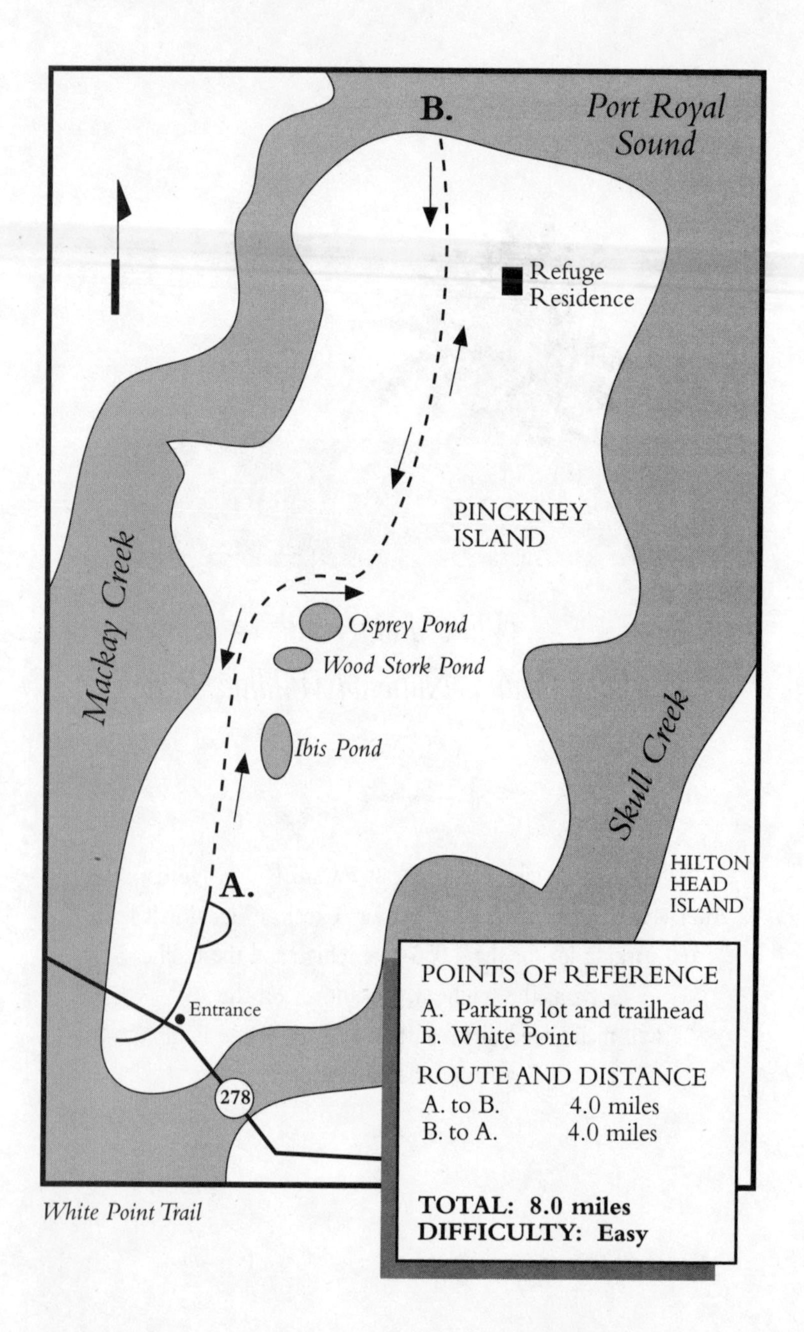

White Point Trail

The Earliest Spring

In midwinter, Pinckney Island rises low and green from the confusion of gray water and brown marsh that separates Hilton Head from the mainland. Since the island lies in the far southeastern corner of the state, it's a good place to go in February to warm up a little and search for the first signs of spring. It is too early for the waves of herons and egrets and oystercatchers that will pour into the refuge later in the year, but there is still a lot to see on a walk in that month—and no mosquitoes to hassle you while you are about it.

I start the trail to White Point on a fine, sunny morning. The sky is an intense blue; the temperature in the fifties and rising. The track is a dirt road, open only to walkers, bicyclists, and refuge vehicles. It traverses the length of the island, crossing terrain that is as flat as the deck of an aircraft carrier. Much of the refuge is salt marsh, and, depending on the tide, parts of the road are bordered by ankle-deep water or vast mud flats. The spartina that grows in the flats will turn bright green in a month or two but is still wintry brown today. But even in February there's plenty of green, too, for long stretches of the road pass through an evergreen maritime forest made up of sprawling live oaks, tall pines, and palmettos of every size.

Palmettos are some of my favorite trees. My affair with them started when I was a boy. To escape the asphalt-melting heat of summertime Columbia, I would lose myself every Saturday in the dark chill of an air-conditioned theater. There I would watch adventures unfold among the palmetto-like trees of black-and-white jungles. Even today, the sight of a palmetto takes me back to those innocent tropics of yesteryear, to crocodiles slithering into warm, muddy rivers, and elephants trumpeting shrill warnings before their earthshaking charges. So, on this walk, in addition to searching for spring, I hope to sort out the different species of palmettos that grow here.

Palmettos are members of the palm family. Their name comes from the Spanish *palmito*, which means "little palm." Only three palms occur naturally in South Carolina, and all of them can be found on Pinckney Island.

I stop first at a saw palmetto, growing under a scruffy pine, less than half a mile from trailhead. This species, *Serenoa repens*, is a shrub, usually four to ten feet tall. Its large fan-shaped leaves are split into slender, graceful leaflets. The saw palmetto is easy to identify by the sharp, serrated edges of its leaf stalks. Though it is scattered here on Pinckney, *Serenoa* forms dense colonies in Florida that often cover miles of flatlands. My idea of hell is a long hike through a saw-palmetto forest in mid-August. It would shred you, bake you—and bore you to death.

Less than a mile from trailhead, the road enters an evergreen maritime forest of pines and live oaks. Dwarf palmettos are scattered across the shady forest floor. Although the dwarf palmetto (*Sabal minor*) belongs to a different genus of the palm family than the saw palmetto, it closely resembles it but comes without the saw. *Sabal minor* is more common on Pinckney than the tender *Serenoa repens*. In fact, the dwarf palmetto is the hardiest North American palm, and it thrives along the Carolina coast as far north as the Outer Banks.

The third palmetto found on Pinckney can be seen occasionally on the brown hammocks that rise from the black muck of the tidal flats, but it is ubiquitous in the maritime forest. It is the best-known tree in the state, and its image can be seen on the state flag and on the state seal. It is, of course, the cabbage palmetto, the state tree of South Carolina.

The cabbage palmetto (*Sabal palmetto*) can grow to ninety feet, though it is usually a more modest thirty to fifty feet in height. Its trunk is unlike that of any other local tree. It is not covered with bark, nor does it have a growing cambium layer. (The crisscross thatching seen on some palmettos is not bark but the remains of dead fronds.) It is made up, instead, of a mass of tough parallel fibers which give it great strength and resilience. The cabbage palmetto's leaves are huge, up to seven feet long and nearly as broad, and, like *Serenoa* and *Sabal minor*, split into long, narrow leaflets. In this forest, the palmettos are short and scattered beneath the towering pines and spreading live oaks. But as

usual they transform the landscape for me, adding tropical romance and the possibility of steamy jungle adventure.

Beyond the maritime forest, the land opens up. I pass fields and patches of forest filled with slash, loblolly, and longleaf pines; red maples and hickories; and sycamores and sweet gums. Yaupons and wax myrtles join scrub palmettos in the understory, and the herbaceous layer is thick with ferns. Near the turnoff to Wood Stork Pond, I spot the first clue that spring might be on the way; thistles about to bloom line the sides of the road.

Pinckney's profusion of plant life and habitats attracts an assortment of birds, especially waterfowl and waders. Nineteen species of ducks have been counted here. On this walk, I have already seen white ibises, great egrets, snowy egrets, and little and great blue herons wading in the tidal flats. But my sightings only hint at Pinckney's bird life. During an earlier trip to the island, I spoke with Layne Hamilton, the refuge manager. After I finished reciting the birds I had seen, she asked me how I missed the wood storks, ospreys, oystercatchers, and bald eagles.

Just beyond the trail that leads to Wood Stork Pond, the road passes through a nearly pure stand of longleaf pines, followed by a mixed stand of slash and loblolly pines. It then reenters the maritime forest. Under tall pines, Spanish moss clings to live oaks, and resurrection ferns, lush and green after a recent rain, carpet the trees' huge branches. A light northerly wind rattles the fronds of the palmettos, and their pleasant music follows me all the way to the tidal creek that crosses the island a half mile from White Point. Though high tide is near and the trail is soggy, it is still passable, and I am soon standing on the sandy point that marks the end of the island.

Low parallel ridges of gray seaweed have washed onto the sand and curve gracefully around the point like elevation lines on a topographic map. The air has a sharp, salty smell mixed with the sweet odor of decaying vegetation.

Three bufflehead ducks swim in the blue-gray waters of Port Royal Sound, and a cormorant suns itself on a navigation marker. I sit down to wait for the largest mammals in these parts to show themselves. I am confident they will appear; I have been coming to these islands for years, and I have seldom missed seeing dolphin. This trip is no exception; within minutes, dorsal fins break the water, and three dolphins porpoise lazily toward the point.

These are bottle-nosed dolphins (*Tursiops truncatus*), the familiar inshore dolphin of the Atlantic coast. The common dolphin (*Delphinus delphis*) is equally widespread, but it is a deep-water creature and rarely comes near shore. "Flipper" was a bottle-nosed dolphin.

Perhaps because they are large, carnivorous animals that appear to be friendly, a special relationship has developed between people and dolphins, a love affair that started with the Greeks four thousand years ago. Since then, dolphins have been painted, studied, mythologized, played with, and trained to seek out deadly mines suspended in the sea. People swim with them, communicate with them, marvel at them, love them, and, as a byproduct of today's highly mechanized fishing industry, slaughter them—in the case of some species almost to extinction. The connection between man and dolphin is complex, more intimate than our association with most other non-domestic animals. And through the years, this special bond has led many writers to wade cheerfully into the warm sea of anthropomorphism. An early example comes from Pliny the Elder, writing about 77 A.D.:

> The dolphin is an animal that is not only friendly to mankind but is also a lover of music, and it can be charmed by singing in harmony, . . .

A more recent example comes from Mrs. Yvonne M. Bliss of Stuart, Florida, who in 1960 fell from a boat near Grand Bahama Island. She believed she survived the accident because she was helped by a dolphin that was in the neighborhood. She described her experience as follows:

> After another eternity and being thankful that my friend [a dolphin] was keeping away the sharks and barracuda for which these waters are famous, the porpoise moved back of me and came around to my right side. I moved over to give room to my companion and later knew that had the porpoise not done this, I would have been going downstream to deeper and faster moving waters. The porpoise had guided me to the section where the water was most shallow.

The use of the words *friend* and *companion* and *guided* by Mrs. Bliss leaves little doubt that she considers the dolphin to be motivated by friendship. It is possible, of course, but most scientists believe dolphins simply like to push things with their noses. In this case, Mrs. Bliss happened to be the thing pushed and shoreward happened to be the direction she was pushed.

The three dolphins in front of me swim effortlessly. Their sleek muscular backs gleam in the sun as they rise gracefully in the water to breathe. Suddenly, two of them leap clear of the water. Since they are less than forty feet away, I know they must see me. And though I'm more scientist than romantic, I would like to believe they are saying hello. I suppose there is a little of Mrs. Bliss in all of us.

During the walk back, I realize what I haven't seen: aside from a few fields kept clear by the refuge manager, there is little sign that human beings ever lived on Pinckney Island. It is not surprising that the Cusabo Indians, who were here when the first

Europeans came, left no scars; their agriculture was organic, their fields small, and their crops similar to the native plants. But early in the eighteenth century, the island was acquired by Charles Pinckney. Later it became the second home and farm of his son Charles Cotesworth Pinckney. In the latter's hands, the island produced a harvest far more valuable than the Indians' corn and pumpkins. Pinckney raised cotton, a crop that enriches its owner as it depletes the soil. And the cotton grown on Pinckney Island was of a particularly enriching variety—long-staple cotton.

Long-staple, or Sea Island, cotton was developed on Hilton Head Island at the end of the eighteenth century. Its fibers are, on average, one inch longer than ordinary cotton. The longer fibers allow it to be spun into finer threads. The result is a fabric that is lighter, silkier to the touch, and considerably more expensive. The fortunes of many low-country families were built on that one inch.

But Charles Cotesworth Pinckney was already a wealthy lawyer when he retired to live part-time on his eponymous island. He had been prominent in state politics and had represented South Carolina at the Constitutional Convention. In 1804 and 1808, he unsuccessfully ran for president on the Federalist ticket. (Thomas Jefferson beat him badly in the first election; James Madison did likewise in the second.) Pinckney was also an enthusiastic, if undistinguished, officer in the Revolutionary War.

In June 1776, fifty British ships appeared off Charleston. Two forts guarded the entrance to the harbor: Fort Johnson to the south and a half-built log fort to the north, on Sullivan's Island. Captain Charles Cotesworth Pinckney was assigned to Fort Johnson, while Colonel Moultrie commanded the troops on Sullivan's Island. On June 28, the British attacked Sullivan's Island.

Only the two sides of the fort facing the water were finished.

The walls were made of logs of the unassuming palmetto. For hours, the British bombarded the half-finished fort. The tough, fibrous palmetto logs took all the punishment that the armada hurled at them. All day long, without splintering and without breaking, they absorbed the pounding, protecting the men in the fort and allowing them to blast away at the British fleet. Although other things went wrong for the British that day, there is little doubt that the fight put up from the unfinished fort of palmetto logs was an important factor in the decision of the British to depart Charleston the next morning, leaving the city, for the time being, in Patriot hands.

As consequences of the battle, a palmetto tree was placed in the center of the state flag, Colonel Moultrie was promoted to general, and the log fort on Sullivan's Island was named after him. Charles Cotesworth Pinckney, who badly wanted to be a part of the action, spent the decisive day at Fort Johnson, far from the fighting. And with no real combat experience he was overlooked by his superiors for important missions and battles during the rest of the war, becoming a bit actor in a conflict in which he had hoped to play a starring role.

Today, all signs of Charles Cotesworth Pinckney—and the family members who inherited the property after his death in 1825—have disappeared from the island. Pinckney's house on White Point was destroyed in an 1824 hurricane, and all traces of the cotton plantations, which prospered under his family's management until the Civil War, are gone. In a reversal of the normal flow of events along this development-happy coast, the maritime forest is reclaiming land. This is one battle that nature is winning. And what could be a more fitting symbol for this victory than the durable palmetto? Not the image on the flag and the state seal but the real thing, growing wild in the maritime forest.

Though the sun is bright and the weather is warm, I am almost back to trailhead before I find an unmistakable sign of spring. Near the side of the road, in the top of a leafless sweet gum, sits a strikingly iridescent, male boat-tailed grackle and a duller-colored female.

Boat-tailed grackles are found throughout Florida, but outside of that state, they stay near the coast. Although they will eat almost anything, they prefer the small fish, shrimps, and insects found in brackish and salt water. Boat-tails are easily distinguished from the common or purple grackle by their larger size and longer tails. It is from this splendid, glossy tail that the bird gets its name; it is creased in flight, and its V-shape resembles the keel of a boat.

Boat-tailed grackles have had lots of names hung on them through the years, and some folks have had a hard time deciding which one was best. It has not been a problem for the locals; since the eighteenth century, boat-tails in South Carolina have been called jackdaws. In this case, it was the scientists who were confused. In 1949, *South Carolina Bird Life* listed the jackdaw as *Cassidix mexicanus westoni*. Nine years later, in *Life Histories of North American Blackbirds, Orioles, Tanagers, and Allies*, the jackdaw had become *C. mexicanus torreyi*. These days, the bird has been redesignated as *Quiscalus major*, and though the ornithologists seem to have finally settled on that name, I'm not sure they've got it right yet. *Quiscalus* is Latin for "quail," so the boat-tailed grackle becomes the "big quail." Now, a fine, strutting boat-tail no more resembles a quail than a peacock resembles a partridge; so, thanks anyway, but I'll stick with jackdaw.

Jackdaws are year-round residents on Pinckney, but the one I'm watching in the sweet gum knows the season is spring. He is bobbing his head, fluffing his feathers, and quivering his wings at the indifferent female a few feet away. Every so often, he throws back his shiny black head, stretches his neck toward the sky, and lets loose with a mad, guttural whistle, the gracklian equivalent of a howl at the moon. And when the female flutters to a new branch a few feet away, he quickly follows. It may be winter in the rest of the state, but on Pinckney Island it's spring.

BEFORE YOU GO

For More Information

Pinckney Island National Wildlife Refuge is administered by The Savannah Coastal Refuges Office of the United States Fish and Wildlife Service. Contact

Savannah Coastal Refuges
P.O. Box 8487
Savannah, Ga. 31412
(912) 652-4415

Accommodations

Hotels, motels, and condominiums to suit every taste and pocketbook are available on Hilton Head. Contact

Hilton Head Island Chamber of Commerce
P.O. Box 5647
Hilton Head Island, S.C. 29938
(803) 785-3673

Campgrounds

Camping is not permitted at Pinckney Island National Wildlife Refuge. The nearest public campground is at Hunting Island State Park, eighteen miles north of Pinckney as the crow flies but about forty miles by car.

Maps

The free trail map of Pinckney Island, which is available at a gazebo in the refuge parking lot, is adequate for this walk.

Special Precautions

During high tides and/or very wet weather, the tidal creek

near the northern tip of the island may flood parts of the trail, cutting off White Point from the rest of the island. I once had to wade 100 feet of the trail in ankle-deep water, but refuge manager Layne Hamilton says she has seen it deeper than that.

Additional Reading

"The Cabbage Palm" by Susan Cerulean, *Florida Wildlife* 46, September/October 1992, 34-37.

Charles Cotesworth Pinckney by Marvin R. Zahniser, University of North Carolina Press, Chapel Hill, 1967.

"Dolphins in Crisis" by Kenneth S. Norris, *National Geographic* 182, September 1992, 2-35.

The Dolphin in History by Ashley Montagu and John C. Lilly, William Andrews Clark Memorial Library, University of California, Los Angeles, 1963. The quotes from Pliny the Elder and Mrs. Bliss were excerpted from passages in this book.

A Founding Family: The Pinckneys of South Carolina by Frances Leigh Williams, Harcourt Brace Jovanovich, New York, 1978.

Hilton Head: A Sea Island Chronicle by Virginia C. Holmgren, Hilton Head Island Publishing Company, Hilton Head, 1959.

Life Histories of North American Blackbirds, Orioles, Tanagers, and Allies by Arthur C. Bent, Dover Publications, Inc., New York, 1965. This book was originally published in 1958 as Smithsonian Institution United States National Museum *Bulletin 211*.

South Carolina Bird Life by Alexander Sprunt, Jr., and E. Burnham Chamberlain, University of South Carolina Press, Columbia, 1949.

Whales, Dolphins, and Porpoises of the World by Mary L. Baker, Doubleday & Company, Inc., Garden City, New York, 1987.

FOREST, BEACH, AND JETTY

Huntington Beach Trails
Huntington Beach State Park

The entrance to the 2,500-acre Huntington Beach State Park is on U.S. 17, 3 miles south of Murrells Inlet, directly across from Brookgreen Gardens.

From the entrance road, drive north to the Marsh Boardwalk parking lot. The trail starts on the east side of the road. The well-marked path follows the shoreline of Sandpiper Pond for most of the 1.2-mile walk to the north picnic area. From there, a short trail leads through the dunes to the beach. Proceed north on the beach to the jetty.

Return on the beach for 4 miles to a marked path through the dunes that leads to the main campground. Follow the signed trail from the campground back to the Marsh Boardwalk.

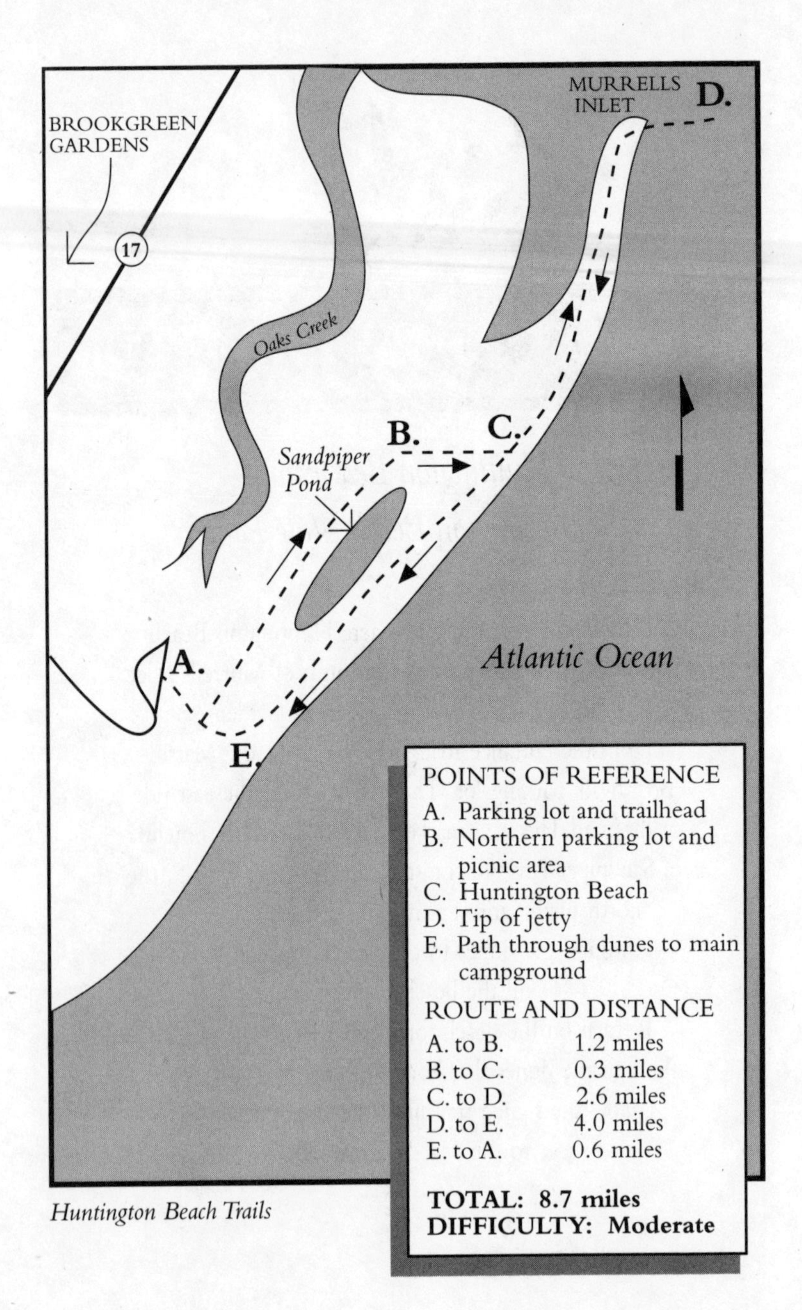

Huntington Beach Trails

Forest, Beach, and Jetty

To tame the shifting shoals and capricious offshore breakers that often made passage through Murrells Inlet hazardous, the United States Army Corps of Engineers built two enormous rock jetties there in 1980. The jetties parallel one another and extend well out to sea, defining and protecting the inlet. At high tide, the north jetty is a jagged ridge of rocks, beginning and ending in water, but the south jetty, which starts at the north end of Huntington Beach, can be reached on foot. To accommodate fishermen, the jetty was topped with a narrow strip of asphalt. The result is a 3,400-foot-long path into the sea that allows hikers to temporarily enter the watery realm of saltwater fish and offshore birds.

I have picnicked on and fished from this jetty many times, and before I took this walk, I revisited the park and strolled out on the jetty. From the end of the paved walkway, Murrells Inlet looked like a broad, dark river. But to the south, the water was shallower, and the sea lightened to a clear Caribbean-like turquoise over the white sand bottom. The tide was slack, the surf calm, the sun warm, the mood serene, but just beyond my feet was a reminder of rougher days. The last few yards of walkway were split into ragged, black strips. A monster surf had smashed into the huge boulders that anchor the jetty, and their bumping and grinding had shredded the asphalt topping. As anyone who lives along this shore could tell you, the weather here is not always tranquil.

Old-timers still remember Hazel, the hurricane that traumatized the South Carolina coast in 1954. They recall the parade of late-model cars arriving from the tony suburbs of Columbia the day after it hit, driven by worried-looking men heading for Pawleys or Myrtle or Cherry Grove to check on their cottages and property. But to young people, Hazel is folklore; when they talk about hurricanes, they talk about Hugo.

Hugo roared ashore near Charleston on September 21, 1989. Winds of over one hundred miles per hour leveled buildings, and flooding ruined many more. Salt spray, whipped into a frenzied foam by the wind, blew across the land, damaging millions of trees and killing many of them. Although areas closer to Charleston were hit harder, Huntington Beach was not completely spared. Bleached crags are visible in the park's maritime forest, and fallen trees litter the forest floor. But hurricanes are as much a part of this ecosystem as beaches, marshes, and forests, and a closer inspection reveals a resilient land with natural communities that are capable of healing themselves. In some of the harder-hit areas (see the chapter on Cape Romain National Wildlife Refuge) the mending may take decades, even centuries, but the process is well underway at Huntington Beach, and this walk offers an opportunity to observe its progress.

I begin at the marsh boardwalk one morning in early spring. The park is famous for its migrating spring birds, and flocks of birders pack the boardwalks and causeway. Judging from the license plates on the cars, they come from all over the northeastern United States and Canada. Men and women in spiffy tan clothes carry spotting scopes, tripods, and expensive-looking cameras with huge lenses. They aim at alligators sunning themselves on islands in the freshwater marsh and snap pictures of birds. The blur of cars and people makes the park appear crowded, but that impression evaporates after a few steps on the trail. The maritime forest is empty of humans, and the sounds of birds soon replace the sounds of birders.

White flowers carpet the sides of the trail. When Hugo thinned the forest, more sunlight penetrated the canopy and the blackberries have responded, temporarily filling the niche left by pines and oaks. But their day in the sun is almost over. Yaupon and wax myrtle are thick in this forest, and they, too, are edging toward sunlight. There are also signs of the eventual victors in this contest for the sun's rays; pine and cedar seedlings have sprouted among the low-lying blackberry vines. In a few years, these trees will shade out the vines' exuberant growth and relegate the yaupons and wax myrtles to their accustomed role of understory. The forest is unusually rich in cedars. The taller pines caught the brunt of the wind-driven salt spray, and many of them died, while the hunkered-down, salt-resistant cedars in the interior survived. The needles of the cedars at the seaward edge of the forest are brown, their trunks twisted and leaning. But even there, tell-tale wisps of green indicate that life still hangs on in the wreckage.

Two species of cedars grow in South Carolina. *Juniperus siliciola*, the southern red cedar, grows only along the coast, while the eastern red cedar, *Juniperus virginiana*, the most common conifer in the eastern United States, can be found anywhere in the state. The two species are almost identical in appearance, but the crown of the southern red cedar usually has a more ragged look about it. In the field, the only measurable difference between the two is the size of the berries: those of the southern red cedar are slightly smaller, five millimeters in diameter, compared to six to ten for the eastern species.

About halfway to the north picnic area, the trail temporarily leaves the maritime forest and crosses a patch of open ground. I pause to examine the sagging limb of a tattered forty-foot-tall cedar growing on an old dune ridge. Which species is it? This time of year there are no berries, and, even if there were, how could I measure their diameters accurately enough to determine a millimeter or two of difference?

Naturalists often face this kind of problem. Without berries, and the calipers with which to measure them, how do you determine which cedar you are examining? Many naturalists, including me, handle identification problems like this by intelligent guessing. There are some clues: the tree's sagging, scraggly look inclines me toward southern red cedar. The eastern cedar is usually denser, with straighter, less droopy limbs. The sandy soil of the dune ridge is another tip-off. The name *Juniperus siliciola* indicates that the species prefers sandy soils. Neither clue is enough to base an identification on, but taken together, they add up to a good guess. Joe Massey, a botany professor at the University of North Carolina at Chapel Hill, says that if you have an 80 percent chance of being right in a field determination, go for it. And so I do, making the following note: "Southern red cedar—I think."

After a little over a mile, the trail leaves the thick tangle of maritime forest at the north picnic area and passes through the dunes to the beach. The direct sun is a pleasant change from the shade of the forest, and a light, salty breeze blows off the sea. I head north toward the jetty, walking on the hard sand of low tide.

Ring-bills stand idly on the beach, and sanderlings run back and forth, chasing the water's edge like mechanical toys as they probe the sand uncovered by receding waves. Shells crunch under my shoes: oysters, cockles, and jackknife clams; scallops, moon snails, and elegant disks; olives and arks. The shells are not evenly distributed along the beach; the surf has deposited them in low mounds, like middens from the sea. A few shell collectors stand over the piles, backs bent, heads bowed, eyes searching.

At the base of the jetty, I clamber up the rocks to the asphalt walkway. When I first began coming to Huntington Beach, there was no jetty, and the park was segregated. By law or by custom—I'm not sure which—the north end of the park was reserved for blacks. In 1964, the Civil Rights Act outlawed segregation, opening all of the park to all races. It was a turbulent era in the state, one that produced drugged-damaged kids as well as long-needed legislation, but I can't recall a more exciting time than those early, heady days of desegregation, when many of us—black and white alike—believed we were re-creating the South as a color-blind society. The passage of time has proven us overly optimistic and shown us that the South's, and the rest of the country's, racial problems are more intractable than we thought. But they were still good days, and the sight of the jetties, where none existed before, reminds me of the spirited days of the '60s, when the winds of change were blowing across the land.

The water is calm at the end of the jetty. Cumulus clouds hang listlessly in a cerulean sky. Both sea and sky appear lifeless, but nature can change expressions quickly.

Abruptly, two dolphin break the water. They begin angling toward shore, cruising into the placid waters south of the jetty. A speck of white appears high in the sky. A bird spirals down. It has a pointed tail, and the tips of its wings look like they have been dipped in black paint. It swoops lower. About forty or fifty feet above the ocean's surface, the bird's spirals tighten. Suddenly, it is in a spectacular wings-back, beak-first stoop. It vanishes in the sea for a second or two, then bobs up like an oversized white cork fifty or so feet in front of the dolphins. The bird's size, coloration, and reckless dive make it easy to identify; it is a northern gannet, a pelagic wanderer rarely seen from shore in this part of the country.

Gannets (*Morus bassanus*) are goose-sized birds, mostly white, with blue bills, and wingspans of up to six feet. They nest in colonies on the rocky cliffs of the Canadian coast but spend little time there, for these are truly birds of the air and sea. Most of their lives are spent offshore, sometimes hundreds of miles from land. They eat only fish and drink salt water.

In winter, dead gannets occasionally wash ashore along this coast. I have seen them lying on the beach, victims of storms or starvation or oil spills. But this is the first one I've ever seen alive. As I watch, the bird labors into the air, gaining altitude with powerful wingbeats, then resting with short glides before spiraling down again into the water.

Soon, two more gannets appear in the sky. The dolphins reverse course and head back toward the jetty. They are clearly feeding. Six mergansers materialize in the water just beyond the surf. Then, like a winged spear, another gannet plunges toward the sea, a plume of white water marking its entrance. Two laughing gulls fly among the gannets, their maniacal calls adding wild music to the scene. Three more gannets join the crowd, and a huge black-backed gull soars above them.

The mergansers dive in front of the dolphins, and gannets begin hitting the water everywhere. A cormorant surfaces just beyond the jetty, and two loons swim toward the action. The dolphins change direction again, a matched pair of sleek gray backs, now moving side by side to the south.

I can't see what caused this furious burst of activity, but it is likely a school of herring—an important link in the food chain on which all these predators depend. In spring and summer, herring swim along this coast, just beyond the breakers. They travel in huge schools that are so tightly packed they appear as shadows in the water, giant ink stains a foot or two below the surface of the sea.

This school must be moving south because the gannets and dolphins gradually drift away from the jetty in that direction. After a while, the dolphins vanish, but I can see the spiraling, plunging gannets for a long time. Then I begin moving myself, walking back down the jetty to the hard-packed beach, then heading south toward trailhead.

Except for the torn asphalt at the tip of the jetty, I find few signs along the beach that a hurricane ever pounded this coast. A maritime forest repairs itself slowly, and man-made structures do not mend themselves at all, but beaches heal quickly. Tall, healthy sea oats cover the dunes, and all manner of birds go about their business on the beach and in the sky.

People have helped the healing process here; the low wooden fences buried in the sand just above the beach, for example, were built by park employees to stabilize the dunes. But, like the yin and yang legacy of the 1960s, not all of man's work along this coast has been helpful. Towering condominiums, golf courses, and the hordes of vacationers they attract have all but eliminated the native fauna and flora from much of the Grand Strand, the stretch of coast between Cherry Grove and Pawleys Island. This development also pollutes the estuaries, rendering oysters inedible and endangering the spawning grounds of many species of fish, including the herring. And as the estuaries decline, so eventually will the predators—the gannets and dolphins and loons—that feed on the shrimp and fish they produce.

So, along the Grand Strand, as in most other coastal areas of the South, it is overdevelopment, not hurricanes, that truly endanger our parks and seashores and refuges. Despite the temporary damage they do, hurricanes pose no real threat to natural areas; they have been slamming this coast for millennia, and the wildlife and beaches and forests have evolved with them as part of the natural system. That's why Huntington Beach is bouncing back so quickly after a "killer storm" like Hugo. But jetties, condominiums, and pollution are new here, and the ecosystems have not had the required millennia to adapt to them. If we want the natural areas that remain along this coast to survive, we humans will have to do the adapting.

BEFORE YOU GO

For More Information

Huntington Beach State Park
Murrells Inlet, S.C. 29576
(803) 237-4440

Accommodations

Huntington Beach State Park is just south of Murrells Inlet, about halfway between Myrtle Beach and Georgetown. Both towns offer a variety of motels, hotels, and condominiums. Contact

Georgetown County Chamber of Commerce
P.O. Box 1776
Georgetown, S.C. 29442
(800) 777-7705

Myrtle Beach Area Chamber of Commerce
1301 North Kings Highway
Myrtle Beach, S.C. 29577
(800) 356-3016

Campgrounds

The park has two campgrounds with a total of 127 campsites. The north campground is only a few hundred yards from the Marsh Boardwalk, where this walk starts.

Maps

The trail through the maritime forest is new and does not appear on any map. However, the path is well marked and the geography is simple, so the map in the free park brochure is sufficient for this walk.

Points of Interest
Atalaya and Brookgreen Gardens

Huntington Beach State Park is named for Anna Hyatt Huntington and her husband, Archer Milton Huntington. In 1930, the Huntingtons bought 6,635 acres of land on Waccamaw Neck, the watery arm of land between the Waccamaw River and the Atlantic Ocean. They later bought more land on the Neck, bringing their total to 9,127 acres. The Depression-era price for the original tract of land, beachfront and all, was thirty-four dollars per acre.

Mrs. Huntington was a sculptor from Boston; Mr. Huntington a well-to-do patron of the arts from New York. They bought the land for a winter home, hoping that the milder climate would alleviate Mrs. Huntington's "tubercular affliction." The Huntingtons also wanted to develop the property as a garden, an environment in which Mrs. Huntington's work, and that of other American sculptors, could be displayed. They named their purchase Brookgreen Gardens, after a plantation that once stood on part of the property.

The Huntingtons moved fast; shortly after buying the property, they incorporated Brookgreen Gardens as a non-profit company, began work on the grounds, and started wondering where they were going to live. Mr. Huntington's answer to that question was a truly remarkable structure—Atalaya.

Atalaya, the Huntington's winter home off and on for fifteen years, sits just off the beach near the south end of the park. Mr. Huntington designed the house to resemble the Moorish homes that he was familiar with on the Spanish coast.

Atalaya is a one-story, masonry structure with a large open plaza in the center and iron bars over the windows. It looks more like a fort, or a prison, than a home. Historians believe that no architectural drawings were used, that Mr. Huntington worked from memory as he supervised construction. In any case, the house is open to the public, and visitors may make their own aesthetic judgments. But however you feel about the architecture, the house is highly successful in one regard: it is durable. It looks today much like it looked in photographs taken during its construction. And as far as I can tell, Hugo harmed it not one bit.

During World War II, Army Air Corps troops were barracked at Atalaya, and after the war, the debilities of old age allowed the Huntingtons only two more winters at Brookgreen. Five years after Mr. Huntington's death in Connecticut in 1955, Mrs. Huntington, realizing that she would never again visit Atalaya, had Brookgreen Gardens lease the house and 2,500 acres of land to the state of South Carolina for use as Huntington Beach State Park. The lease was for fifty years, and it cost the state one dollar.

Brookgreen Gardens proper lies just across U.S. 17 from Huntington Beach State Park. It is home to an impressive array of sculptures, botanical gardens, wildlife parks, and some of the biggest live oaks in the state. Mrs. Huntington died in 1973 at the age of ninety-seven, but her work lives on at Brookgreen. Its best-known piece, the fifteen-foot metal statue, *Fighting Stallions*, at the entrance to the gardens, was based on one of her clay sculptures.

Brookgreen Gardens is open every day except Christmas. For information, contact Brookgreen Gardens, Murrells Inlet, S.C. 29576, (803) 237-4218.

Additional Reading

Archer Milton Huntington by Beatrice Gilman Proske, The Hispanic Society of America, New York, 1963.

The Audubon Society Encyclopedia of North American Birds by John K. Terres, Wings Press, New York, 1991. This book was originally published by Alfred A. Knopf and was last copyrighted by them in 1980.

Huntington Beach State Park: A Visitors Guide to the Historic and Natural Features by Ray Sigmon, Mike Foley, and Mark Barker, South Carolina Department of Parks, Recreation, and Tourism. This twenty-two-page booklet is on sale at the convenience store in the park. Much of my account of the history of Brookgreen Gardens was excerpted from it.

BIRDERS' PARADISE

Bulls Island Trails
Cape Romain National Wildlife Refuge

The 34,229 acres of islands and water that make up Cape Romain National Wildlife Refuge are located 20 miles north of Charleston. Bulls Island is the most developed part of the refuge, and the most accessible. A ferry to the island leaves from the refuge boat dock at Moores Landing. To reach the dock from U.S. 17, take SeeWee Road east for 4 miles, then go right for 1 mile on Bulls Island Road. It is a half-hour ferry ride from Moores Landing to Bulls Island. From the ferry dock on Bulls Island, a dirt road leads 0.3 mile to a rest area, which has drinking water, restrooms, and picnic tables. From the rest area, follow Beach Road a few hundred feet to a maintenance station; an unmarked trail near the station angles off to the right toward Summerhouse Ponds, passes between the upper and lower ponds, and ends at Beach Road. Cross Beach Road to Lighthouse Road to begin the loop around the eastern end of the island. Complete the loop on Old Fort Road, which will return you to the rest area. From there, retrace your footsteps to the dock.

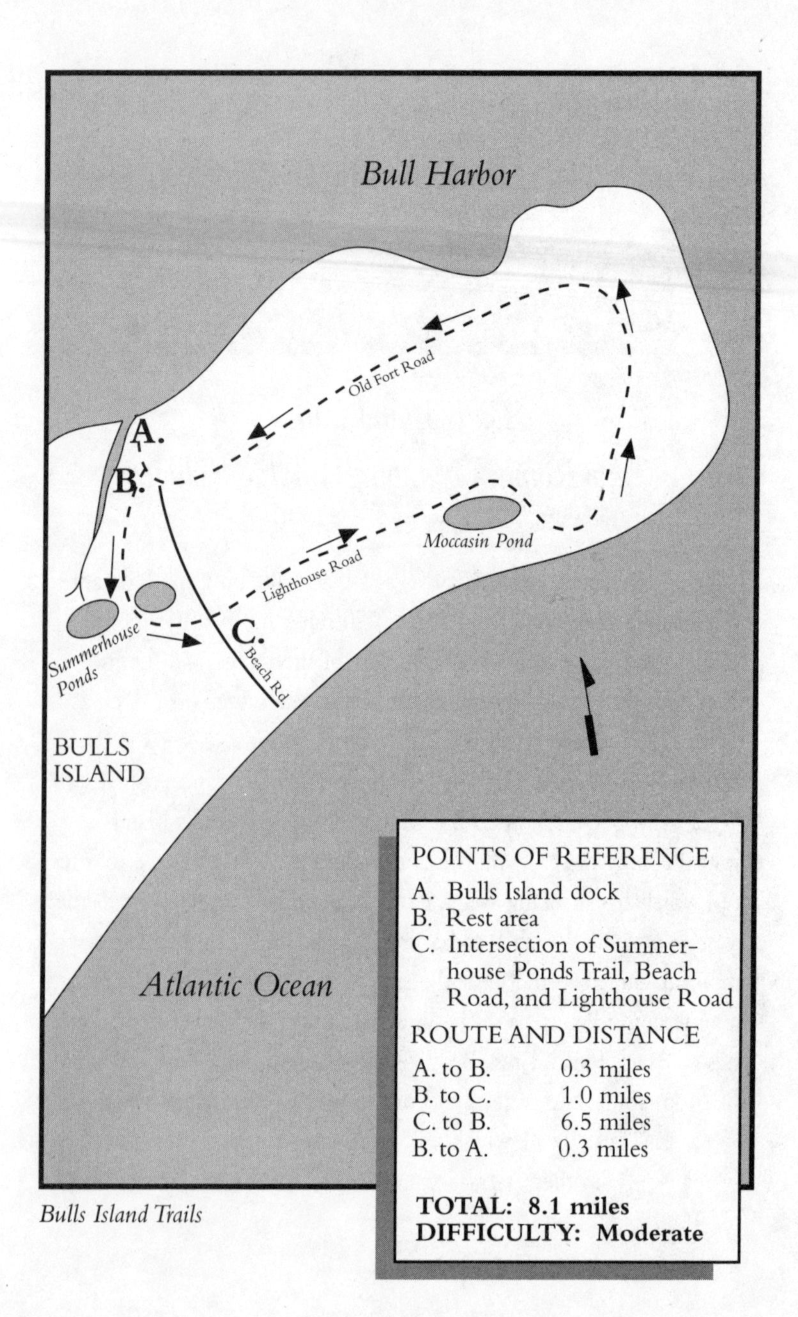

Bulls Island Trails

Birders' Paradise

Unlike Huntington Beach, which was only grazed by Hurricane Hugo, Cape Romain felt the storm's full fury. Winds of 135 miles per hour sent a twenty-foot-high surge of salt water crashing over Bulls Island, inundating all but the highest ridges. The storm devastated the island, reducing its once luxuriant maritime forest to a few tattered trees, a lot of waist-high brush, and acre after acre of oaks and pines with their tops snapped off twenty or thirty feet above the ground. The result is a landscape many consider ugly, a forest just beginning to re-create itself.

But ugliness, like beauty, is in the eye of the beholder, and some beholders love Cape Romain's ravaged terrain. Many plants and animals are flourishing in the new environment, and the populations of some birds—woodpeckers, mourning doves, and wild turkeys, for example—are higher since the storm. Because of the plentiful birds, another species also finds the island irresistible; birders from all over the United States congregate at Cape Romain. And during one sunny spring day, it was my good fortune to join Lee Grant, an old friend from Texas and one of the more enthusiastic members of *Homo birdus americanus*, on my first visit to the refuge.

Lee is a compact, medium-sized, middle-aged man with cropped brown hair. Today, he is wearing his usual birding outfit of lightweight hiking boots, jeans, khaki shirt, a Dallas Cowboys baseball hat, and a sunburn from a previous expedition. He is friendly, outgoing, and humorous—except on birding expeditions, when he becomes quiet and intense. Lee loves birds, loves to find them, loves to identify and make notes about them. He is a *very serious* birder.

We start at the Bulls Island boat dock, accompanied by fifteen or so binocular-draped shipmates who rode over with us on the morning ferry. During the boat ride, Lee took notes. After the short walk to the rest area, he hands me his small black notebook. I read his tidy handwriting:

- Brown pelican
- Double-crested cormorant
- Snowy egret
- Great egret
- Great blue heron
- Little blue heron
- Green heron

- Clapper rail
- American oystercatcher
- Semipalmated plover
- Black-bellied plover
- Killdeer
- Whimbrel

Since Lee doesn't seem interested in my notes, I read them to myself:

> Most of the trees in what was once a maritime forest are now bleached white by the sun, like skulls in a Georgia O'Keeffe painting. A few palmettos, live oaks, and small cedars are still standing, but the island resembles a war zone. Even so, I like its stark beauty. Going to be a fine walk.
>
> Deer tracks all over the road and doves flying along the edge of the marsh.

Departing the rest area, we angle right, leaving Beach Road for the trail to Upper and Lower Summerhouse ponds. A few huge live oaks are still standing near the road, a hint of the pre-Hugo forest. The trail leads to a broad, sandy causeway between the two ponds. Most of our fellow passengers have remained near the rest area, so Lee and I are alone on the causeway. We see alligators and a black snake four or five feet long. Lee breaks his normal birding silence to tell a story about a large, aggressive gator that once ran him off a path at a refuge in Texas. I stop to watch a small alligator whose eyes barely show above the surface of Upper Summerhouse Pond. Lee glances at the gator, mutters something inaudible, and hurries up the trail.

The American alligator (*Alligator mississippiensis*) is the largest reptile in North America, occasionally exceeding eighteen feet in length. Along the east coast, alligators range from southern

Florida to North Carolina's Albemarle Sound. Gators are more plentiful in the southern part of their range, but they are not uncommon these days in coastal South Carolina.

When Europeans first arrived in the South, they began killing alligators for their hides, for meat, and because they plain didn't like them. By 1964, the number of gators in South Carolina was so low that the hunting season had to be closed, and in 1973, *A. mississippiensis* was placed on the list of endangered species. The gators responded well; populations grew rapidly, and the species was removed from the endangered list in 1987. By 1993, the number of gators in South Carolina had grown to one hundred thousand, and the state was toying with reopening its hunting season.

One of the things about alligators that fascinates me is their longevity as a race. Alligators are crocodilians, a group that first appeared two hundred million years ago, about the time of the earliest dinosaurs. Over the ages, dinosaurs evolved into hundreds of species from the agile, meat-eating *Tyrannosaurus* to the huge, lumbering, vegetarian *Brontosaurus*. Then, of course, they became extinct. Crocodilians, on the other hand, have stayed pretty much the same. Even today, after millions of years in which to diversify, only three families and twenty-one species make up the order Crocodylia. That this stuck-in-the-mud order survived, while the dinosaurs didn't, has always struck me as curious.

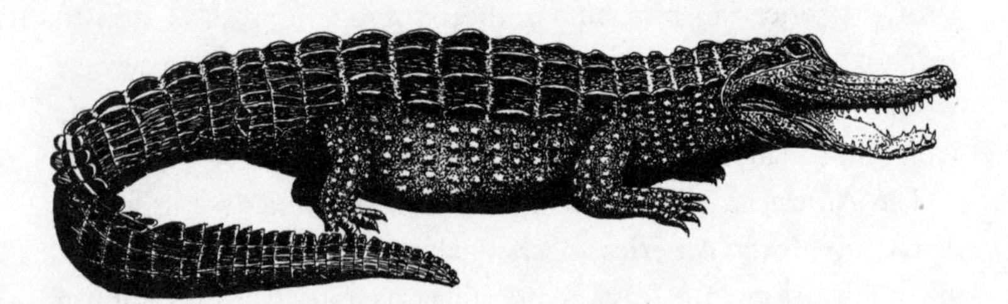

Like all creatures, crocodilians evolved to fill an ecological niche. Even though the planet has changed dramatically since they first appeared, they've stayed, essentially unchanged, in that niche. To achieve that kind of stability, they must be doing something right, and in the case of alligators, I believe I know what it is.

Alligators lead the kind of low-waste, low-impact lives that deserve our attention. Like all crocodilians, alligators are cold blooded. So, unlike mammals, they don't have to expend energy maintaining a constant body temperature. When alligators want to warm up, they lie in the sun; when they want to cool down, they lie in the shade or in water. It's a simple, efficient, low-energy lifestyle—which means that gators don't have to eat very often. In fact, during cold weather, alligators don't eat at all, routinely going six months between meals.

When an alligator does eat, though, it gets the most out of its food. Gators have very acidic stomachs that can digest almost anything, from turtle shells to bird feathers. As a consequence, alligators can and will eat almost anything. They have been observed chowing down on rats, rabbits, ducks, muskrat, fish, and small deer. They eat dogs, turtles, shellfish, snakes, and an occasional person.

In Florida, between 1973 and 1988, six people were killed by alligators. These tragedies were awarded sensational headlines and long stories on the evening news. But before running out to buy a gun to waste a gator or two, consider the news that gets no headlines: Florida loses almost three thousand people *a year* in automobile accidents, and, in the country as a whole, fourteen hundred more die in firearm accidents. In fact, the chances of killing yourself accidentally while driving to a local gator hole with a gun in the car are far greater than the chances of the gator getting you. In the wild, in fact, most alligators treat humans just like the one I'm watching does: they ignore you for a while, then silently slide away and vanish in dark water.

Beyond the ponds, the trail narrows and enters a patch of thick brush. The terrain is dry and sandy. Lee stops often to search for birds with his binoculars and to make notes. After we cross Beach Road to Lighthouse Road, he reads his notes aloud:

- Short-billed dowitcher
- Sandpiper (species unknown)
- Laughing gull
- Little tern
- Royal tern
- Black skimmer
- Turkey vulture
- Black vulture
- Red-tailed hawk
- Red-headed woodpecker

I look over my own notes:

> It's hot and getting hotter, and thanks to Hugo, there is no shade. But if the trees have suffered, some of the wildlife—like the birds Lee is always stopping to look at—have benefited. So has the underbrush—yaupon, smilax, and poison oak are everywhere. Some of the live oaks are starting to come back, too; there's a fringe of green on some trees that must have looked dead until recently. Perhaps hurricanes play a role in this ecosystem similar to the one fire plays in the longleaf pine-wire grass ecosystem. Perhaps in some way we don't yet understand, periodic hurricanes are necessary to perpetuate a maritime forest.
>
> Deer tracks and doves are everywhere.

We continue east on Lighthouse Road. A massive osprey nest sits high in a snag near the road. An osprey chick peers over the edge of the nest. The chick's parents become more and more agitated the closer we get to the nest, so we hurry by to avoid disturbing them further.

The road passes Moccasin Pond. A boardwalk that once extended into the pond lies crumpled and broken on the shore. Beyond the pond, near the beach, is a totally devastated area. For as far as I can see, every tree, except for a few palmettos, has been uprooted or snapped in two. The landscape is surreal, more desert than forest. We pause, momentarily stunned by the destruction, then head north across the island, paralleling Boneyard Beach, a name that seems particularly appropriate in the post-Hugo era.

The road takes us between a mud flat and a freshwater marsh. Snake and alligator tracks form lazy sine waves in the sand of the road, and overhead, in a cloudless blue sky, a boat-tailed grackle harasses a red-tailed hawk. A big alligator lies quietly in the still waters of a shallow pond in the marsh to our left. The mud flat is filled with birds; Lee stops to identify them but regularly turns his head to keep an eye on the gator.

Beyond the mud flat, the cross-island road intersects Old Fort Road, and we proceed west to Old Fort itself. What remains of the structure is a tabby wall a few inches high and about three hundred feet in circumference. It is not clear when Old Fort was built nor what it was used for, though suppositions abound. Nor is it clear why the Society of First Families of South Carolina chose this spot to erect a sign commemorating the first landing of European settlers in the state.

According to historian Lewis Jones, British settlers on the ship *Carolina* first landed at SeeWee Bay in 1670, between modern McClellanville and Mount Pleasant, on their way to found Charles Town. Nobody knows exactly where the 1670 expedition came ashore, but it is certain that Old Fort was built long after the original settlers passed through. So why put the sign here, next to Old Fort? The proximity of the two seems to imply a connection where none exists.

From Old Fort, we slog down a wide dirt road. Lee stops often to study the woodpeckers and flycatchers he spots along the way. I urge him along, hurrying now to get back to the rest area. When we arrive, we sit on a picnic table in the shade of a massive live oak. Lee flips through his notes, jots something down, and reads his final entries to me:

- Red-tailed hawk
- Osprey
- Mourning dove
- Red-bellied woodpecker
- Pileated woodpecker
- Eastern kingbird
- Great-crested flycatcher
- Barn swallow
- American crow
- Wood thrush
- Northern cardinal
- Red-winged blackbird
- Common grackle
- Orchard oriole
- Boat-tailed grackle
- Total 38 species. Could have done better, but for some reason Manning wanted to hurry.

Then, for the first time, I read my notes to him:

> No shade at all on Old Fort Road. Tired of stark beauty. Tired of being philosophical about Hugo. Hate what that damned storm did to the island. Would trade all of Lee's great-crested flycatchers for a cold beer. Would probably trade all of the great-crested flycatchers in South Carolina for a cold beer. Might throw in the woodpeckers, too.
>
> Rabbit tracks everywhere. Lots of red-tailed hawks and doves.

"We'll have a beer later," Lee says. "It's tally time now. Number of species?"

I look through my notes. "Two."

"That's it? Two? All those notes you've been scribbling, and all you got was two species. I thought you were trying to make a living at this."

"I was studying the ecosystem as a whole, trying to determine what Hugo did to the maritime forest. I wasn't just looking for birds."

"People are interested in birds," Lee says, "not maritime forests."

"I never saw the forest before Hugo tore it up," I say. "But I hear it was a magical, beautiful place."

"Keep your day job," advises Lee.

It's easy to long for the disappeared forest of Bulls Island, easy to regret that I won't live long enough to see it reestablish itself, as it indeed will, given a chance. After the storm, refuge personnel widened the roads on the island to act as firebreaks, planted a little rye grass and clover and lespedeza, but otherwise decided to stand by and watch the island regenerate itself. The process is underway, but it will take a century or two for the maritime forest, the part of the ecosystem most damaged by the storm, to reach its previous lushness.

Already, however, the island's deer—60 percent of which were killed in the storm—are coming back, as the brush, upon which they browse, flourishes in bright sunlight that once could not penetrate the forest canopy. Mourning doves, which feed on seeds made plentiful by the growth of weeds and planted grasses, are ubiquitous. George Garris, the refuge manager, says that marsh rabbits and cotton rats are also much more abundant today than before Hugo. In fact, the hurricane helped those organisms that prefer a more open environment—the plants and animals of the edge—because Hugo has created an island that is almost all edge.

Besides the edge lovers, the storm also benefited the red-tailed hawks and gators and snakes—predators that feed on edge lovers. But as the forest reassembles itself, the island will move toward its old equilibrium. Fast-growing loblolly pines will shade out the burgeoning browse, and the number of deer and marsh rabbits and red-tailed hawks will ebb; wood warblers will wax as the mourning doves wane. *H. birdus americanus* may also decline as the forest closes in, and easy-to-spot species give way to the secretive birds of the deep woods.

Maybe. Maybe all of the above will happen. But nature is complex, and the answers to ecological questions are rarely simple. Causal connections are hard to establish. Like the conjunction of Old Fort and the sign commemorating the landing of the *Carolina*, putting two facts side by side tempts one to assume a relationship where one doesn't necessarily exist. The reasons for the growth of the deer herd, for example, might include a number of factors unrelated to the increase in browse, though that increase has almost certainly played a role.

The truth is, no one knows exactly what is going to happen on Bulls Island, or when. A grand experiment is underway here, one that may shed some light on the role hurricanes play in these ecosystems. Though I will not be around to see much of the results, with a little luck, my children and grandchildren will be. And, hopefully, so will the gators. They've already outlasted the dinosaurs, and if we don't get too liberal with our hunting seasons, they'll probably outlast us, too.

BEFORE YOU GO

For More Information

Cape Romain National Wildlife Refuge
5801 Highway 17 North
Awendaw, S.C. 29429
(803) 928-3368

Accommodations

The closest lodging is in the Mount Pleasant–Isle of Palms area. For information, contact

Charleston Trident Convention & Visitors Bureau
P.O. Box 975
Charleston, S.C. 29402
(803) 853-8000

Campgrounds

Camping is not permitted in the refuge. The nearest campgrounds are in Francis Marion National Forest. For information, contact

Francis Marion National Forest
Wambaw Ranger District
P.O Box 788
McClellanville, S.C. 29458
(803) 887-3257

Maps

The map in the Cape Romain brochure is insufficiently detailed to use as a trail guide, but an 8½ x 11-inch map of Bulls

Island is available on request from the refuge. The map is free and suitable for this walk.

Special Precautions

Water, restrooms, and picnic tables are located at the Bulls Island rest area. There are no other facilities on the island. Since the ferry to Bulls Island leaves Moores Landing at 9 A.M. and doesn't get back to the mainland until 4:30 P.M., visitors will spend most of the day on the island, so take food and anything else you expect to need. During warm months, sun block and DEET are indispensable.

Although there is little to fear from the alligators of Bulls Island, it is prudent to keep a respectful distance between you and them, especially if "them" is a big gator. Children and dogs are attacked more frequently than adults, so be especially cautious if they accompany you.

Additional Reading

"Alligators" by David Lee, *Wildlife in North Carolina* 57, May 1993, 8-12.

The Alligator's Life History by E. A. McIlhenny, Ten Speed Press, Berkeley, California, 1987. This odd, fascinating book was originally published in 1934. It is based on the author's 60 years of observation of alligators near his home at Avery Island, Louisiana. If the author's name and address seem familiar, it is because they are printed on every bottle of Tabasco sauce. Avery Island is where the peppers are grown, and the McIlhennys are the family that turn them into that wonderful, fiery sauce.

"Gator!" by Nancy Coleman Wooten, *South Carolina Wildlife 15*, July/August 1992, 12-15.

South Carolina: A Synoptic History for Laymen by Lewis P. Jones, Sandlapper Publishing, Inc., Orangeburg, South Carolina, 1971.

BESIDE A TIDAL CREEK

Indian Mound Trail
Edisto Beach State Park

Edisto Beach State Park is 50 miles southwest of Charleston. From U.S. 17, take S.C. 174 south for about 25 miles. The main entrance to the 1,255-acre park is on S.C. 174, at a sharp bend where the road turns southwest and begins to parallel the beach. Trailhead for the Indian Mound Trail is 0.2 mile west of S.C. 174 on State Cabin Road, which is 1 mile north of the main entrance. From a parking area, the trail enters a maritime forest of bays, dwarf palmettos, and live oaks. After 0.1 mile the trail forks, with the Indian Mound Trail continuing left. At 0.4 mile, the trail forks again, beginning a short loop. Stay left and follow the southern leg of the trail to Scott Creek and the Indian shell mound. On your return, complete the loop by proceeding straight ahead at the fork where the southern leg of the loop goes to the right.

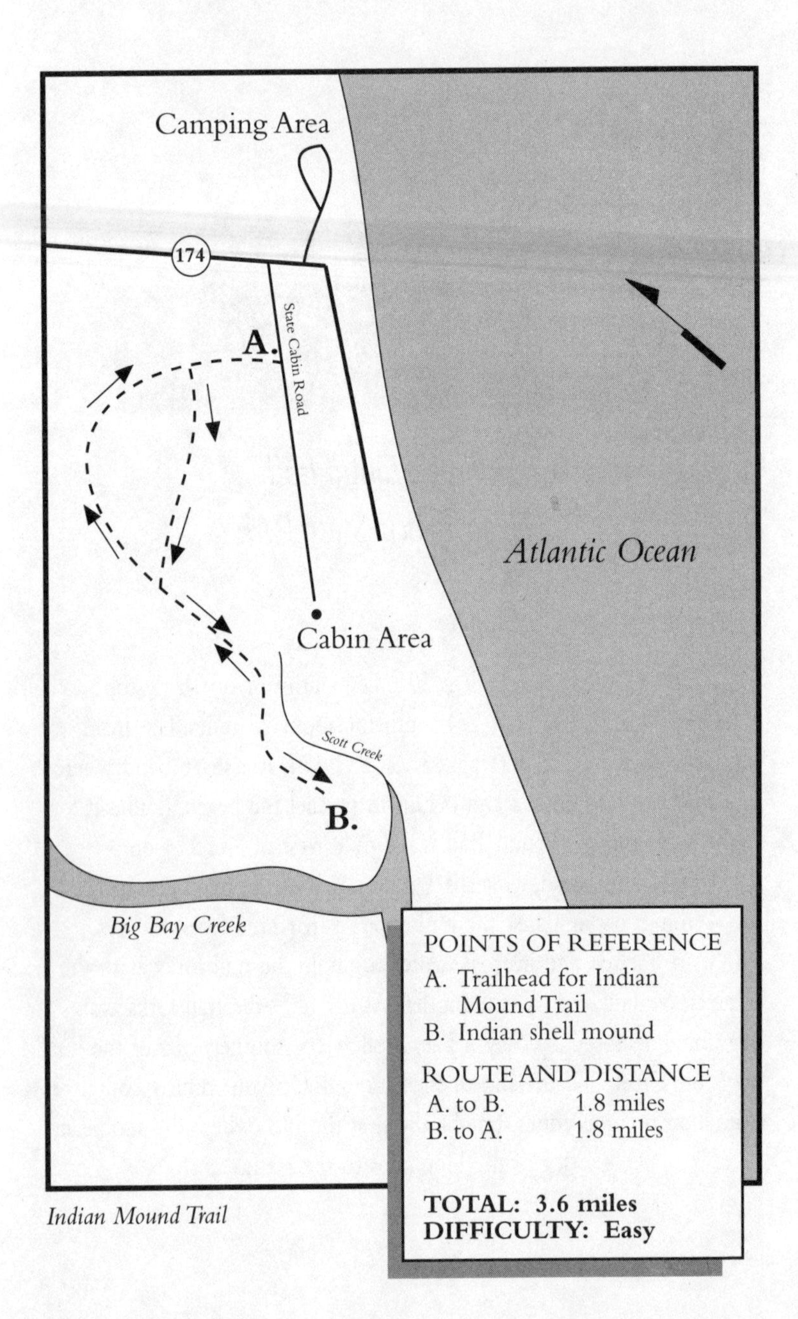

Indian Mound Trail

Beside a Tidal Creek

Edisto Island is a ragged thumbprint of land bordered by the North and South Edisto rivers, the Atlantic Ocean, and the Intracoastal Waterway. Profusions of rivers and creeks etch watery whorls across the island. Many of these waterways are guarded by the mansions of early planters, who began settling the island in the seventeenth century and eventually grew rich on indigo and sea-island cotton. But the southernmost stream on Edisto, Scott Creek, remained untouched (as far I can determine), until 1935 when the Civilian Conservation Corps began building a park between the north side of the creek and the ocean. Today, the part of Edisto Beach State Park that most visitors see is a sparkling one-and-a-half-mile-long white-sand beach, civilized with restrooms, picnic shelters, and a campground. But north of Scott Creek, in a less-developed section of the park, the Indian Mound Trail passes through lush forests and dazzling green marshes, where you can still get a whiff of Edisto's shadowy pre-colonial past.

Diane and I start the trail on a warm morning in early May. The broad track is soft and brown with live oak leaves that have dropped from the huge trees that overhang the trail. Loblolly pines and cabbage palmettos and sweet gums are scattered among the oaks; wild grapevines and Virginia creepers climb over small trees in the understory. Bright-green ferns line both sides of the path. The only thing missing is a sign that says "Classic Southern Maritime Forest."

The trail forks a few hundred yards from trailhead, and the Indian Mound Trail bears left. The path narrows and enters a dense forest that includes water oaks and willow oaks, along with the ubiquitous live oaks. The air is fragrant with the smells of cedars and bays, and with the sweet, heavy odor of honeysuckle. Brilliant-red, trumpet-shaped wildflowers bristle from three-foot-tall spikes beside the path. Diane identifies them as coral bean (*Erythrina herbacea*), a plant she remembers from her childhood in Florida.

Members of the genus *Erythrina* are common in the tropics and in our southwestern deserts, but they are rare in South Carolina. *E. herbacea* is an exception; it can be found along the coast as far north as North Carolina, though it becomes increasingly uncommon in the upper part of its range. Coral bean, also known as Cherokee bean, gets its name from the shiny, hard, bright-red seeds it produces. In Florida, where the plant is common, children string the seeds on threads and wear them as necklaces, which is why Diane remembers the plant so well. She also remembers being told that the seeds are poisonous, a fact my field guide confirms.

Although most plants and animals rely on camouflage or flight to avoid being eaten, bad-tasting or bad-smelling or poisonous ones often advertise themselves. The skunk's white stripe means "I don't have to hide, so back off, Buster." The ominous sound of a rattlesnake carries a similar warning. The bright color of coral-bean seeds (which are so deadly to rodents that Mexicans mix them with peanut butter to use as rat poison) must transmit the same cautionary message to the golden mice and wood rats of the maritime forest. These rodents could easily reach and eat the seeds of this low-lying plant. However, unlike birds, whose short digestive tracks generally protect them from the seeds' poisonous effects, rodents almost invariably digest (and destroy) them. Since mice and rats and coral beans are all still abundant in the state's coastal forests, the seeds' bright-red warning must work. But no protection is perfect, and many coral-bean seeds never sprouted because they ended up on necklaces or in lethal concoctions for rats.

Indian Mound Trail continues east along the edge of a marsh. It crosses a tidal creek, green with spartina, then reenters the forest. The tall palmettos, the tangles of vines, and the dense understory look more like an illustration from *The Jungle Books* than a South Carolina park. Brilliant-green dragonflies flit among the plants, searching for insects and reinforcing the exotic atmosphere.

Only a mockingbird perched in a magnolia reminds us that we are still in the South.

Scott Creek finally comes into view, and the trail parallels it, dipping in and out of the forest. A scattering of yuccas appear on the higher ground, each plant separated from its neighbors by ten feet or more. I rub my fingers along the edge of a leaf; the tiny teeth identify it as an aloe yucca, usually, and more descriptively, called Spanish bayonet. The mound lily yucca, a similar species, also occurs in South Carolina, but its leaves are not edged with teeth.

Like the coral bean, Spanish bayonet (*Yucca aloifolia*) is a plant of the tropics, though similar species are also found in the southwest. *Y. aloifolia*, a member of the lily family, is an evergreen with stiff, eighteen-inch-long, blade-shaped leaves, tipped with sharp spines. Touch the tip of one, and you will understand immediately how the plant got its common name. The spines protect the yuccas from grazing animals, but, like the coral bean's poison, the device isn't perfect; an analysis of the dung of an extinct ground sloth in the southwest showed that 80 percent of its diet was the leaves of the Joshua tree, the biggest, spiniest yucca of them all.

Spanish bayonet has a flower stalk that can reach six feet in height. The white flowers are large and showy and produce a pulpy, cylindrical fruit containing small, black seeds. Birds eat the fruits and spread the seeds, which might account for the spacing between the plants.

A breeze comes up off the river. Doves coo in the distance, and a cardinal sings in a tall loblolly pine. A red-bellied woodpecker flies over the path and begins hammering a tree. The trail narrows again, then ends abruptly at a sign near a vegetation-covered mound, about fifteen feet tall and forty feet in diameter.

The mound is called Spanish Mount. It was named for the earliest European explorers of the island, although they did not create it. According to the sign, it is one of the larger middens on the South Carolina coast—and one of the oldest. Archeologists have determined that some of the pottery shards from the midden came from clay vessels that are four thousand years old.

No one knows what the people who created this midden called themselves, nor have archeologists assigned them a name. The purpose of the midden itself is equally murky. Was it a garbage dump? A place to gather and eat oysters and tell stories? A site for ceremonies or a place to fire pottery?

We poke around the midden. Partially-buried oyster shells protrude from the dirt. One side of the mound has been undercut by water and drops sharply to Scott Creek. Diane finds a few pottery fragments on the shore of the creek. They are small and unremarkable in every way except one: a human hand has decorated each piece with neat rows of indentations by pressing a reed or, in one case, a periwinkle into the clay before it was fired. The markings are so characteristically human that they could have been made by a modern-day potter, and handling them produces an unmistakable tingle of kinship.

On the side of the mound farthest from the sign, I find a seat among the yuccas and dwarf palmettos. Below, the blue-gray waters of the creek wind lazily through green marsh. It soon becomes obvious that I am sitting in a natural blind. Barn swallows sweep over the water in front of me, pelicans and laughing gulls pass overhead, and a summer tanager flies to a windswept cedar beside the mound. Three common terns—graceful white birds with black caps and black-tipped orange bills—plunge over and over again into the creek. They enter the water beak first, then quickly pop to the surface and into the air, usually with a small fish between their mandibles. I am happy to see these terns. Although they are still abundant over much of their range, their numbers have been dropping in some parts of the country.

The common tern (*Sterna hirundo*) has never been very common in South Carolina, at least not south of Charleston. They usually breed farther north and winter farther south. So these birds are likely just passing through, stopping off for a bite to eat on their way north. All terns are agile flyers, and the common tern, sometimes called the "sea swallow," is no exception. Their aerial skills help them escape hungry hawks and falcons, but proved useless against the guns of plume hunters, who had almost wiped out the species by 1905, when laws were finally passed to stop the slaughter.

Terns are members of the family Laridae, as are gulls. Gulls and terns resemble one another in coloration (mostly white bodies, with gray or black mantles) and in their affinity for water. But the kinship doesn't go much deeper than that. In fact, the greatest threat to the common tern today is the sea gull, good old Jonathan Livingston himself, the romanticized white buzzard of the sea. Gulls raid the terns' nesting colonies, devouring unattended eggs and chicks. There's nothing new about this; gulls have preyed on tern nesting sites for centuries, and the two long ago established a normal predator-prey balance. That balance is changing today, however, because of the exploding gull population.

Unlike terns, which eat fish almost exclusively, gulls have developed a taste for garbage. Herring gulls and ring-bills scream over tidbits of food in landfills throughout their range. As human populations near lakes and seacoasts have increased, so have the number of garbage dumps—and the number of gulls. Thus, the recent decline of the common tern can be traced to its other nemesis—us. And as before, its aerial proficiency isn't going to help it much.

The walk back from the mound is as flat and easy as the stroll in. We lengthen our strides and enjoy the simple, rhythmical act of walking. After a few minutes, the trail forks and we go left to complete the northern half of the loop. It's drier here, with fewer big trees and thicker understory. Sassafras and yaupon grow beside the path, and brown thrashers and blue jays flash through the underbrush. The guttural *ka-ka-ka* of a yellow-billed cuckoo comes from deep in the woods. A slender, head-high oddball of a tree stands a few feet from the trail. Its leaves cling to the tips of twigs that sprout from the top of an unbranched trunk. I think I know what it is, but I gingerly wrap my hand around it to be sure. I pull back when I feel the thorns on the trunk. It is *Aralia spinosa*, all right, the aptly named Devil's-walking-stick.

A. spinosa is a member of the ginseng family. One of its relatives is the herb ginseng or "sang," from whose roots the Chinese make a tea believed to be an aphrodisiac. Ginseng is difficult to cultivate, so Americans began exporting wild sang to Asia early in the eighteenth century and continue to do so today. The roots of *A. spinosa*, on the other hand, were used in home remedies for headaches. Because drug companies now manufacture a plethora of headache cures but good aphrodisiacs are still hard to come by, Devil's-walking-stick can be found all over the state but wild ginseng is quite rare.

After the two legs of the Indian Mound loop rejoin each other, the trail curves south beneath a living arch of live oak branches. The oaks and occasional loblollies here are huge, the understory vibrant with growth. This looks like virgin forest, but the history of this land is obscure and no one knows for sure. In any case, if it was ever logged, it happened a long time ago.

The trail ends among some small pines and bays. A mockingbird sits in a sweet gum above our car. His songs ring out defiantly. I wonder if the trail we just finished follows the same route that those unnamed people took four thousand years ago to reach the site now called Spanish Mount. Although books have been written about the history of Edisto, they invariably start with the arrival of the planters. Consequently, we know much about those early settlers and their slaves and their creek-side mansions, but almost nothing about the people who created the midden on Scott Creek. We know only a little more about the Edistows themselves, the Indians for whom the island is named.

The first humans reached South Carolina fifteen thousand years ago. They roamed the state with the mammoths and mastodons, but left behind only a few stone axes and scrapers to help us decipher their lives. The people associated with Spanish Mount came to Edisto over ten thousand years later, in a period that saw the first pottery-making along this coast.

By the time the Spanish arrived at Parris Island in 1566, the Cusabo Indians, a confederation of tribes on South Carolina's southern coast, were hunting deer with bows and arrows and supplementing their kills with corn and beans and squash. A few years later, one of the Cusabo tribes, the Edistows, relocated from St. Helena Island in Port Royal Sound to an island in the Bay of Orista, the island now known as Edisto. The reason for their move is unclear, and in fact, only one historian (Chapman J. Milling in *Red Carolinians*) mentions it. Nobody mentions the people, if any, whom the Edistows displaced on the island.

After their move, the Edistows went into a tailspin. The reasons were the usual ones: a war with another tribe, European diseases, and ongoing conflicts with the early settlers. Their spears and arrows were as useless against European disease and blunderbuss

as the terns' graceful wings were against plume hunters, or the yuccas' spines against the ground sloth. Evolution had not prepared them for the white man, and long before the Revolutionary War, the Edistows were gone from Edisto. Not much later, the entire Cusabo confederation had vanished.

It is tempting to compare the fate of the mound builders with that of the Edistows, to speculate that some event occurred—perhaps an invasion by a more warlike tribe who decided to relocate, as the Edistows did—that was as catastrophic to them as Europeans were to the Edistows. But the pottery shards don't tell us how the story ends, and the final chapter in the history of the people of Spanish Mount remains as shadowy as the purpose of the midden that stands beside Scott Creek.

BEFORE YOU GO

For More Information

Edisto Beach State Park
8377 State Cabin Road
Edisto Island, S.C. 29438
(803) 869-2756

Accommodations

Five vacation cabins are tucked away in the park, in the woods along Scott Creek. They are usually booked well in advance. For reservations, contact Edisto Beach State Park.

There are no motels or hotels on Edisto Island, but numerous rental cottages and condominiums are available. For information, contact

Edisto Chamber of Commerce
P.O. Box 206
Edisto Island, S.C. 29438
(803) 869-3867

Campgrounds

Seventy-five campsites are located near the beach in the main section of the park. Some of these can be reserved; others are available only on a first-come, first-served basis. For information, contact the park.

Maps

The map in the free park brochure is all that's needed for this well-marked trail.

Fees

A $2.00 day-use fee is charged at the main gate, but entrance to the section of the park that lies north of Scott Creek—where the Indian Mound Trail is located—is free.

Special Precautions

In late spring and summer, deer flies and mosquitoes can be a problem along Indian Mound Trail; that is, they will eat you alive and strip the flesh from your bones in seconds. Long pants, a long-sleeved shirt, and a gallon or two of insect repellent are a must in the warm months.

Additional Reading

The Common Tern by Joanna Burger and Michael Gochfeld, Columbia University Press, New York, 1991.

Early Pottery in the Southeast: Tradition and Innovation in Cooking Technology by Kenneth E. Sassaman, The University of Alabama Press, Tuscaloosa, Alabama, 1993.

Edisto: A Sea Island Principality by Clara Childs Puckette (with Clara Childs Mackenzie), Seaforth Publications, Cleveland, Ohio, 1978.

"An Island in Time" by Emily E. Clements, *South Carolina Wildlife* 40, July-August 1993, 22-33.

Life Histories of North American Gulls and Terns by Arthur Cleveland Bent, Dover Publications, New York, 1963. This book was originally published in 1921 as Smithsonian Institution United States National Museum *Bulletin 113*.

Red Carolinians by Chapman J. Milling, The University of North Carolina Press, Chapel Hill, North Carolina, 1940.

South Carolina: A Synoptic History for Laymen by Lewis P. Jones, Sandlapper Publishing, Inc., Orangeburg, South Carolina, 1971.

South Carolina Bird Life by Alexander Sprunt, Jr., and E. Burnham Chamberlain, University of South Carolina Press, Columbia, 1949.

South Carolina: The Making of a Landscape by Charles F. Kovacik and John J. Winberry, University of South Carolina Press, Columbia, 1989.

THE COASTAL PLAIN

Cypress is not an Evergreen with us, and is therefore called the bald Cypress, . . . These Trees are the largest for Height and Thickness, that we have in this part of the World; some of them holding thirty-six Foot in Circumference.

John Lawson, 1709

A CYPRESS-GUM SWAMP

Boardwalk Loop
Francis Beidler Forest

Francis Beidler Forest, a National Audubon Society sanctuary, is located 40 miles northwest of Charleston, just north of I-26. The entrance to the 5,820-acre forest is on S.C. 28, which can be reached from U.S. 178 about 7 miles southeast of Harleyville.

All of this walk is on a handicapped-accessible boardwalk that loops through the heart of Four Holes Swamp. The first leg follows the northern segment of the loop, starting at the visitor center and proceeding 0.8 mile to an overlook on Goodson Lake. The return leg follows the southern portion of the loop.

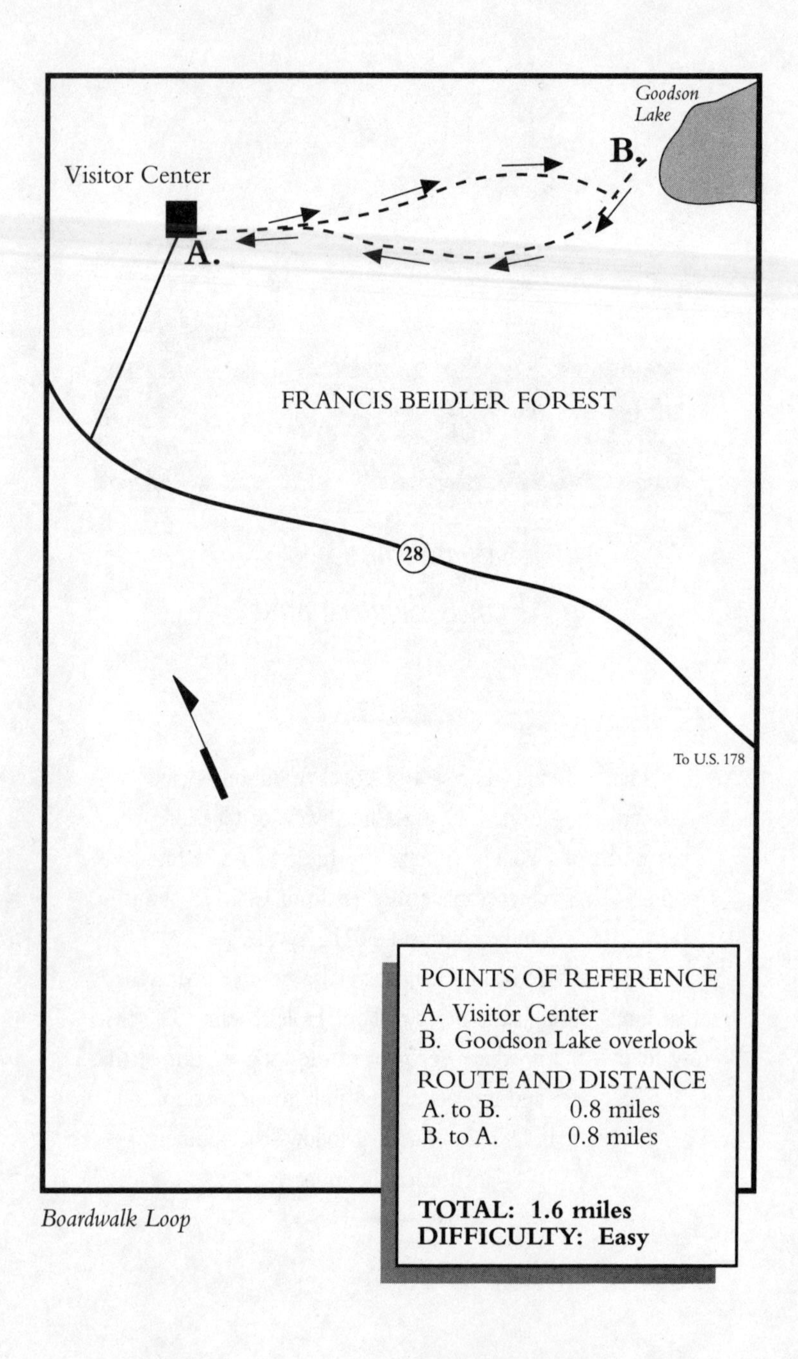

Boardwalk Loop

A Cypress-Gum Swamp

When I mentioned to my barber that my next walk was in a swamp, George stopped snipping and said with some passion that maybe I wasn't too smart. He said that he doesn't like swamps, and when he thinks of them, which isn't very often, bad smells, stagnant water, and—lowering his voice ominously—slimy venomous snakes are what come to mind. I asked him if he'd ever been to a swamp. He said no, then suggested in a kindly way that maybe I should look for a healthier occupation.

A lot of people react similarly to swamps, but I love them. I like the diversity of life—the turtles sliding by in still, black waters, the towering trees rising out of a morning mist, the festoons of Spanish moss swaying in a breeze. And when I think of swamps—which, unlike George, *is* rather often—I think of Francis Beidler Forest. It is a picture-perfect wilderness and the quintessential swamp.

Francis Beidler Forest is an Audubon Society sanctuary located in the heart of Four Holes Swamp. A boardwalk runs eight-tenths of a mile from the sanctuary's visitor center to Goodson Lake. It passes through the centerpiece of the sanctuary, a 1,763-acre virgin bald cypress-tupelo gum forest, the largest remaining tract of its kind in the world.

I start the boardwalk trail on a cool, overcast autumn day. Aided by a breeze, the hardwoods are shedding their leaves. As they drift down and strike other leaves, they make a gentle patter, like a light rain falling in the woods. Leaves litter the boardwalk, adding splotches of color to the weathered gray planking. The forest is thick with sweet-smelling shrubs and trees. Ironwoods, wax myrtles, sweet gums, and oaks rise up beside the boardwalk, while dwarf palmettos and Christmas ferns hug the ground on either side. A hairy vine of poison ivy, as thick as my forearm, clings to the trunk of a water oak.

An emerald-green lizard with a yellowish stripe down its back climbs a post near the water oak and peers over the boardwalk rail. It is a Carolina anole (*Anole carolinensis*), a reptile that can be found anywhere in the state but is quite common in the coastal plain. Its color indicates that it is angry.

Anoles are not true chameleons, but they share with them the ability to change colors. Unlike chameleons, anoles do not change colors to blend into a background; they do it to regulate their temperature and to express themselves. On a cool, gray day like this, an anole would normally be brown, a color that would enable it to better absorb sunlight and stay warm. Since this one is green, I suspect that it is a male in a fighting mood, perhaps because another anole has encroached on its territory. Or maybe he thinks I'm the trespasser. As I walk toward him, his skin seems to glow even greener. Finally, he scoots down the post and disappears under the boardwalk, hopefully to relax and change to a warmer brown.

Farther down the boardwalk, the first cypresses and tupelo gums appear. A huge down cypress with a section of collapsed boardwalk lying beside it is a reminder that Hurricane Hugo passed this way a few years back, and though the Audubon Society has repaired the boardwalk, they left the rest of the forest to recover naturally. Surprisingly little damage from the hurricane is still evident, and most of the cypresses, stabilized by their buttressed trunks and interlocking system of roots and knees, weathered the storm.

One South Carolina naturalist told me she cried on seeing the devastation Hugo wreaked in the state's natural areas, but with the exception of Cape Romain and Francis Marion National Forest, both of which took a direct hit, most of the signs of the worst hurricane to slam South Carolina in decades are gone. As Yellowstone has bounced back from the fires that were supposed to have "destroyed" it, so South Carolina has recovered from Hugo. Fires and hurricanes have regularly visited North American ecosystems for centuries, and after years of trying to fight them and clean up after them, we are now learning to live with them. For some people, this was (and still is) a difficult transition—a sea change in attitude—but many natural areas appear to be thriving because of it.

The boardwalk soon enters a dark, swampy area. Sharp-pointed cypress knees protrude from a shallow sheet of sluggishly flowing black water. The huge, swollen trunks of bald cypresses support small crowns 120 feet above the water. Scattered among the cypresses are tupelo gums, trees that occasionally reach one hundred feet in height but are mere understory in this forest.

Cypresses are the glamour trees here, so the tupelo gum (*Nyssa aquatica*) is often overlooked. Though its cousin, the black gum (*Nyssa sylvatica*) is distributed throughout the state (and in the drier parts of Four Holes), the tupelo gum is found only in deep swamps. Like the cypress, *N. aquatica* usually has a buttressed trunk and a narrow crown. But even in winter, when both species have lost their leaves (or their needles in the case of the cypresses), tupelo gums are easy to distinguish from their neighbors because their lower branches are twisted into odd, angular, sometimes drooping shapes.

As a timber tree, the tupelo gum is far less valuable than the cypress, which produces durable, rot-resistant, high-priced lumber. Wood from the tupelo gum is light, soft, and weak, usable only as furniture veneer or pulpwood. No one in their right mind would drain a swamp to log tupelos. So, in addition to Francis Beidler, the conservationist and lumberman who bought this land in the 1890s and never got around to logging parts of it, I believe we owe a small debt of gratitude to the tupelo gum. Its presence made logging the swamp less profitable and may have helped Beidler—and later his heirs—justify their decision to spare this forest.

I follow the boardwalk deeper into the swamp. Fall is the dry season here, and the fringes of the sanctuary are dry. But here in the middle of the swamp, water is everywhere. It is not stagnant water; Four Holes is a forest flooded by shallow creeks. The hydrology is similar to that of the Everglades, where—before it was channeled—a 50-mile-wide sheet of water flowed from Lake Okeechobee to Florida Bay during the rainy season. Of course, the creeks that flow through Four Holes are not that broad, but in the wet season, they can still inundate a one-and-a-half-mile-wide flood plain.

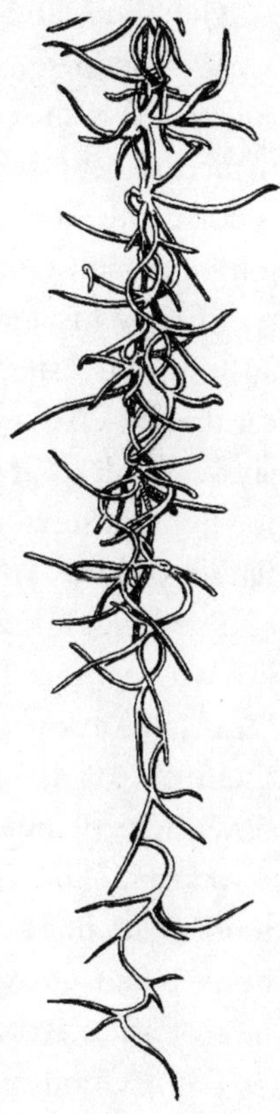

The boardwalk ends at an overlook on Goodson Lake, a long black pond overhung with hardwoods and cypresses and Spanish moss. Goodson is not really a lake but a deep pool in one of the creeks. Many such "lakes" exist in the swamp. Some of them, like Goodson, are partially spring fed, and they remain wet, even in the driest seasons. The pools serve the same purpose here that gator holes do in the Everglades; they provide a year-round home for creatures that must have water to survive—the fish and turtles and river otters, all of which thrive at Goodson Lake.

As I step onto the wooden platform that overlooks the lake, a great blue heron explodes from the water and flaps heavily into the forest. On the far shore, a half dozen yellow-bellied sliders sun themselves on a log. A dragonfly sails down the center of the creek, and a persistent bird calls *fee-bee, fee-bee, fee-bee* over and over again from a nearby tree. I sit down on a bench and try to spot the singer with my binoculars.

The bird I am listening to is an eastern phoebe (*Sayornis phoebe*), a year-round resident in the mountains of South Carolina, and a fall and winter visitor to this part of the state. The onomatopoetically named phoebe is easily identified by its sharp, distinct call, which is fortunate because its grayish color blends perfectly with the foliage around Goodson Lake, making it almost impossible to see.

I finally locate the phoebe in a gum tree forty feet away. It is an undistinguished sparrow-sized bird, lighter on the breast than on the back. It is gazing intently at the lake—or rather at the air above the lake. It's not just taking in the scenery, it is searching for flying insects, proper behavior for a member of an aggressive family of birds known as tyrant flycatchers.

The kingbird, a summer inhabitant of Four Holes, is the best-known member of the family. It is famous for attacking larger birds (and in one spectacular case a low-flying airplane) to drive them out of its territory. Compared to kingbirds, the phoebe is downright demure, even tame. In *Life Histories of North American Flycatchers, Larks, Swallows, and Their Allies,* Arthur Cleveland Bent reports an incident in which a phoebe, driven, I suppose, by hunger and an excess of good will, pecked mosquitoes off the face of a hunter as he waited on a deer stand.

From Goodson Lake, I start my return to the visitor center by way of the southern portion of the boardwalk loop. It takes me back into the heart of the swamp, past water-tolerant cypresses and tupelo gums and water ashes. I pass a bald cypress that is twenty-one feet in circumference and is estimated to

be one thousand years old. Its massive trunk is surrounded by knees, which are partially submerged in shallow black water. A dried ring of liverworts around the base of the tree shows the normal high-water mark that the creek reaches in the wet season—about three feet above today's level. I stop to peer into the water.

Four Holes is called a black-water swamp, and the water does indeed appear to be black. But it isn't; it is actually a clear light brown, often described as tea colored. It looks black because the organic muck at the bottom of the swamp is black. The brown color in the water comes from tannin, a complex mixture of plant polyphenols that the slow-flowing water leaches from the swamp's vegetable matter. Like other wetlands, swamps are remarkably good water purifiers. The plants and muck absorb and filter out impurities. The Beidler Forest brochure points out that some of the water flowing beneath the boardwalk here at Four Holes will end up as drinking water for the city of Charleston—after it's treated to remove the tannin.

From the center of the swamp, the boardwalk climbs imperceptibly back toward the visitor center. The first patches of dry land reappear, covered by dwarf palmettos and loblolly pines. Then oaks, elms, and dogwoods show up on the higher ground. I know I'm out of the part of the swamp that is regularly flooded when I pass a black gum, one of my all-time favorite trees.

The black gum, or black tupelo, belongs to the same genus as the tupelo gums of the deep swamp, but it is quite different from its cousin in one important respect. Whereas the wood of the water tupelo is weak and close-grained, that of the black gum is tough, cross-grained, and impossible to split. In *A Natural History of Trees*, Donald Peattie writes that "It [the black gum] is as easy to split across as it is lengthwise—that is, it can't be done at all, even with wedge and sledge."

I don't favor the black gum because of its aesthetic appeal, for it is not a particularly large or handsome tree. It can reach a height of one hundred feet, but rarely does. Its bark is thick and rough and dark, and its trunk is topped with a dense crown of crooked branches. No, I like this tree for reasons that have nothing to do with its appearance; I like it because of a story its toughness inspired.

John Lawson tells the tale in his 1709 book, *A New Voyage to Carolina*. One day in July, Lawson was visiting a village of Tuskeruro Indians. A terrible storm came up, and lightning killed one of the Tuskeruros. The funeral service was conducted the next day by an Indian priest (whom Lawson refers to as "the Doctor"):

> Then the Doctor began to talk, and told the people what lightning was, and that it kill'd everything that dwelt upon the Earth; nay, the very fishes did not escape; for it often reach'd the Porpoises and other fish, and destroyed them; . . . He added that no Wood or Tree could withstand it except the black Gum, and that it would run round that tree a great many times, to enter therein, but could not effect it. Now you must understand, that sort of Gum will not split or rive; therefore, I suppose, the Story might arise from thence.

Who can resist a tree so tough that even lightning won't strike it?

When I reach the visitor center, I sit for a minute outside the door and listen to the sounds of the swamp: an owl hooting in the distance, the wind gently rattling the autumn leaves. I'd like to get George out of his barbershop for a few hours to join me on the boardwalk, to see and smell and hear this swamp. We'd walk past the magnificent cypresses and tupelos and talk about the toughness of black gums. We'd spend some time at Goodson

Lake, listening to phoebes, watching anoles and turtles, and hoping to see the river otters that I missed today. And if we ran into any of the twelve species of snakes that inhabit the swamp—most of which are secretive and harmless—I'd try to explain to him how they, like the hurricanes, are a natural part of this ecosystem and not the loathsome creatures he believes them to be. I'm certain that one walk through Four Holes would change George's mind about swamps—but it might take several to change his mind about snakes.

BEFORE YOU GO

For More Information

Francis Beidler Forest
336 Sanctuary Road
Harleyville, S.C. 29448
(803) 462-2150

Accommodations

A wide choice of motels can be found in St. George, just off I-95, or in Summerville, just off I-26. Contact

Tri-County Regional Chamber of Commerce
5546 Memorial Boulevard
St. George, S.C. 29477
(803) 563-9091

Summerville Chamber of Commerce
P.O. Box 670
Summerville, S.C. 29484
(803) 873-2931

Campgrounds

Camping is not permitted in the sanctuary. The closest public campgrounds are at Givhans Ferry State Park and Santee State Park. For information, contact

Givhans Ferry State Park
Route 3, Box 327
Ridgeville, S.C. 29472
(803) 873-0692

Santee State Park
Route 1, Box 79
Santee, S.C. 29142
(803) 854-2408

Maps

The entire trail is on a well-marked boardwalk; no maps are needed.

Fees

There is a $4.00 admission fee to Francis Beidler Forest. The fee is reduced for children and Audubon Society life members.

Additional Reading

Amphibians and Reptiles of the Carolinas and Virginia by Bernard S. Martof, William M. Palmer, Joseph R. Baily, and Julian R. Harrison III, The University of North Carolina Press, Chapel Hill, 1980.

"The Circus Lizard" by David S. Lee, *Wildlife in North Carolina* 56, May 1992, 24-27.

"Field Trip: Francis Beidler Forest" by Linda Renshaw, *South Carolina Wildlife* 38, March/April 1991, 50-53.

The Great Cypress Swamps by John V. Dennis, Louisiana State University Press, Baton Rouge, 1988.

Life Histories of North American Flycatchers, Larks, Swallows, and Their Allies by Arthur Cleveland Bent, Dover Publications, New

York, 1963. This book was originally published in 1942 as Smithsonian Institution United States National Museum *Bulletin 179.*

A Natural History of Trees of Eastern and Central North America by Donald Culross Peattie, Houghton Mifflin Company, Boston, 1948.

A New Voyage to Carolina by John Lawson, edited with an introduction and notes by Hugh Talmage Lefler, The University of North Carolina Press, Chapel Hill, 1967. This book was first published in London in 1709.

AMONG BIG TREES

Oak Ridge Loop
Congaree Swamp National Monument

The entrance to the 22,200-acre Congaree Swamp National Monument is 20 miles southeast of Columbia, just off S.C. 734 (Old Bluff Road), which can be reached from S.C. 48. From the parking lot at the ranger station, Bluff Trail runs 0.3 mile to a low boardwalk. Take the boardwalk south, then follow the eastern leg of Weston Lake Loop Trail to its intersection with Oak Ridge Trail. Oak Ridge Trail proceeds west and then north to another junction with the Weston Lake Loop Trail. Follow the western leg of the loop trail to an elevated boardwalk which leads back to trailhead.

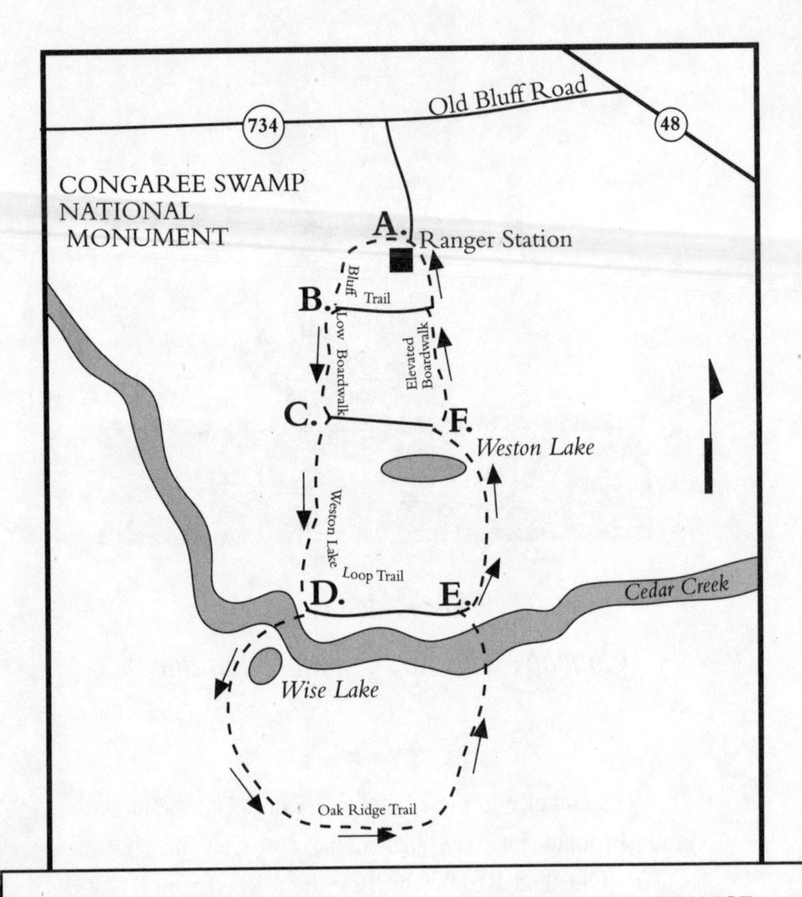

POINTS OF REFERENCE

A. Trailhead for Bluff Trail
B. Intersection of Bluff Trail and Low Boardwalk Trail
C. Intersection of Low Boardwalk Trail and eastern leg of Weston Lake Loop Trail
D. Intersection of Weston Lake Loop Trail and Oak Ridge Trail
E. Intersection of Oak Ridge Trail and western leg of Weston Lake Loop Trail
F. Intersection of Weston Lake Loop Trail and Elevated Boardwalk Trail

ROUTE AND DISTANCE

A. to B.	0.3 miles
B. to C.	0.6 miles
C. to D.	0.6 miles
D. to E.	3.4 miles
E. to F.	1.0 miles
F. to A.	0.9 miles

TOTAL: 6.8 miles
DIFFICULTY:
Easy to Moderate

Among Big Trees

The Santee and its tributary rivers drain almost 40 percent of South Carolina. A molecule of water dripping from a rhododendron leaf into a white-water rivulet near Sassafras Mountain in the Appalachian foothills could wind up entering the Atlantic Ocean at Santee delta, south of Winyah Bay. Along the way, the name we assign to the bodies of water carrying that molecule will change a number of times.

The unnamed rivulet in the foothills flows into the rocky streambed of the upper Saluda, a clear, free-flowing mountain river. After the Saluda enters the

Piedmont, it is slowed by the first of three dams it will encounter on its way to the sea—and is temporarily renamed Lake Greenwood. After passing the dam, the river flows freely again for a brief time before it becomes Lake Murray. Beyond Lake Murray, the Saluda joins the Broad River and takes on yet another name—the Congaree. The waters of the Congaree flow into Lake Marion, and, unless they are diverted by canal into Lake Moultrie and the Cooper River, they will then join the Santee River on the last leg of their journey to the Atlantic.

Much of this great mountains-to-sea watercourse has been subdued—dredged and dammed and channeled—but in one stretch, in the segment we call the Congaree, it still meanders quite a bit, especially during high water. For after the river passes Columbia and enters the flat vastness of the coastal plain, its flood plain widens dramatically in a region where centuries of floods have created a great swamp of oxbow lakes, sloughs, and old channels. In 1976, over fifteen acres of that flood plain were designated as Congaree Swamp National Monument.

Unlike Beidler Forest, whose black-water streams originate in the coastal plain, the Congaree is a brown-water swamp. During the river's passage through the Piedmont, it picks up a load of silt and clay. When wet weather swells the river and floods the swamp, as it does about ten times a year, its muddy-brown waters dump great quantities of nutrients on the flood plain. The result is moist, rich soil, in which some of the largest trees in the state grow.

In 1979, six national and nineteen state champion trees grew in the monument. Hurricane Hugo toppled some of them, however, and larger specimens of several species were discovered elsewhere, so the Congaree claims fewer record trees today. By 1994, it had only one national champion, a forty-six-foot-tall possum haw. But don't let the sparsity of records fool you: big trees still flourish there. And there's no better way to see them than a walk into the interior of the swamp.

I start the Bluff Trail on a warm fall day. Autumn is the dry season here, the season less subject to flooding, and it is an excellent time to hike the Congaree. The leaves are just beginning to change, and flashes of red and gold brighten the dark-green canopy. The trail leads south from the ranger station, through a forest of sweet gums, red maples, and water oaks. Beeches grow to huge sizes on the higher ground, and an occasional loblolly pine towers well above them. Wisps of Spanish moss hang from the trees. In the hush of the forest, a Carolina wren begins its repetitive song.

After a few hundred yards, Bluff Trail intersects a low boardwalk, and I take it farther south, heading into the heart of the swamp. The air at the ranger station was dry, but in here, in the dimness of the forest, it smells damp. Wet spots appear beneath the boardwalk, and after a few more yards, the swollen trunks of water tupelos rise beside the walkway's planks. The tupelos' dark-purple fruits, which resemble elongated black olives, cover the boardwalk. When I squash one between my fingers, I can feel the hard seed inside, and its dark juices stain my fingers.

A loud *whack, whack, whack* rings out in the forest. Three crow-sized, black-and-white birds with blazing red crests are furiously attacking a tall snag fifty feet from me. This is not my first experience with pileated woodpeckers, but I've never seen three of them together—and I've never been this close to one.

The pileated woodpecker (*Dryocopus pileatus*) is a fairly common, permanent resident of South Carolina, and seems to favor swamps, particularly old-growth swamps. Pileateds are big birds, and they need big trees to accommodate their large nesting cavities. They also need the numerous snags found in mature forests.

Pileateds will eat berries, but they prefer grubs and wood-boring beetles and ants, which they find beneath the bark of standing dead trees. To get at these delicacies, they will literally tear a tree to pieces. As I watch, the three birds move quickly around the snag in front of me. Chips of dead wood and bark fly into the air. The activity is frenzied and brief. After a moment or two they move to another snag farther away, and then to a third. They soon vanish, but the dull *whack, whack, whack* continues in the distance for a while longer.

In his 1731 book, *The Natural History of Carolina, Florida, and the Bahama Islands*, Mark Catesby, one of the earliest painters of North American birds, referred to the pileated as "The Larger Red-crested Wood-pecker" and to its slightly bigger, more famous cousin, the ivory-bill, as "The Largest White-bill Woodpecker." Ivory-billed woodpeckers were never plentiful, and their numbers dropped even further as Europeans spread through North America. Rumors of their extinction have been around for years. Since the habits and appearance of the continent's two largest woodpeckers are quite similar, it is not clear why the pileateds held their own, while the ivory-bills waned. Ornithologists have proffered theories ranging from the ivory-bills' overly specialized feeding habits, to increased competition from pileated woodpeckers over the old-growth habitat preferred by both species. In any case, it appears today that the ivory-bill is really gone, and the pileated is now, unfortunately, the "*Largest* Red-crested Woodpecker."

The boardwalk continues into the swamp. The first cypresses appear and, on higher ground, a stand of large red maples and a smattering of ironwoods. A hawk screeches in the distance. The boardwalk bears left, but I proceed straight ahead, moving deeper into the forest on the yellow-blazed Weston Lake Loop Trail.

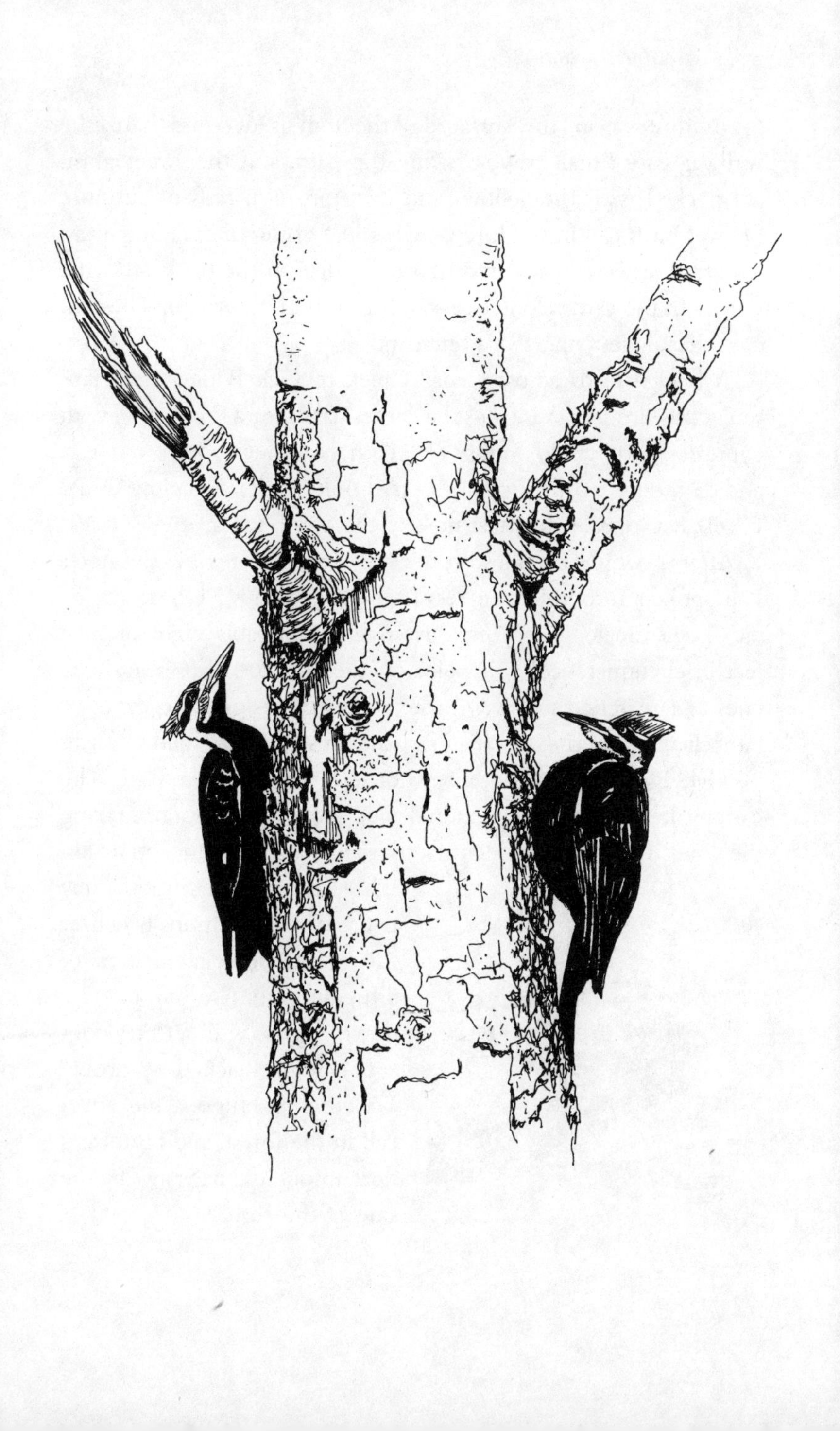

In this season, the surface of the trail is dry and hard, the walking easy. Small pawpaws line the path, and the sweet gums are flecked with the yellows and deep purplish-reds of autumn. Distant birds call in the forest, their songs rising then fading away. The trail leads to a deserted hunting lodge on the bank of Cedar Creek. In the yard, a lone tree stands guard, a huge swamp chestnut oak, the biggest one I've ever seen.

A bridge leads across Cedar Creek to Oak Ridge Trail. This trail curls around Wise Lake, a large, dark pond overhung with cypresses and tupelo gums. The path continues south and east and then turns north, forming a three-mile semicircle below Cedar Creek. It is one of the great trails in the South for trees—*big* trees.

After a couple of miles on the trail, I stop to review the notes I've spoken into my tape recorder. "Big hollies," I hear myself say, "huge tupelo gum," "even *bigger* holly, probably eight or nine feet in circumference." The voice on the tape then lapses into cliches as I searched for even more superlatives: "gigantic cypress," "unbelievable cherrybark oak," "stupendous sweet gum," and so forth.

Oak Ridge Trail continues north toward Weston Lake. The canopy here must be a hundred feet above the ground, making the trees impossible to identify by their leaves. I concentrate on what I can see, the smooth, gray trunk of an enormous beech or the rough, corrugated bark of a tupelo gum. The trail passes a down cypress with a thirty-foot root ball still attached—probably a victim of Hugo. Chickadees call in the forest, and butterflies float among the pawpaws by the side of the path.

Beneath the trees, the understory varies: open and park-like one minute, thick and heavy with vines the next. Tiny white asters and pinkweed bloom beside the trail. On the bank of a surprisingly clear creek, an even more surprising cluster of late-blooming hearts-a-bustin' have just finished flowering. I pass a huge swamp chestnut oak, twelve or thirteen feet in diameter, whose size easily exceeds the previous "biggest swamp chestnut oak I've ever seen." Near the oak, the path reeks of cat urine—almost certainly the territorial mark of a bobcat.

The trail recrosses Cedar Creek and continues north. Along the drier sections of trail, a few ramrod-straight loblolly pines reach well above the hardwoods and grow toward the sun. When I reach the elevated boardwalk, I climb the stairs, find a bench on the overlook, and scan Weston Lake. It is a sizable cypress-rimmed oxbow lake, black and teeming with life. Turtles rest on logs near the banks; minnows and gars swim beneath the overlook. A large, thick fish, over two feet long, cruises by sluggishly, just below the surface of the water. I bend down for a closer look, but I don't need to see the coarse scales on its body or the barbels on its lips to identify it. Its size gives it away. This is a carp, the bad-tasting trash fish that every Southerner has learned to loathe.

But it was not always thus. When they were introduced into this country from Germany in 1877, the carp was hailed as a wonder fish: big, fast growing, and delicious as table fare. Every state wanted carp in their waters. Congress jumped in to help, and in no time at all, carp were flourishing in lakes and rivers from Massachusetts to Florida to California. By the turn of the century, the fish were well established in most states. The reports coming back to Washington, however, were not glowing. Carp, the reports said, displaced the native chubs and suckers, they ate the wild celery and pond weeds on which migrating waterfowl fed, and their bottom feeding ruined highly productive lakes by muddying the water so badly that the resulting turbidity choked off the growth of aquatic vegetation. Not only that, carp were bony, impossible to filet, and tasted, well, yucky.

Most of the reports turned out to be true, so the government began a study to see how they could rid themselves of this pestilence they had once called a "wonder fish." A biologist was hired, and after three years of study, he concluded that carp were, on the whole, indestructible. Learn to live with them, he advised. So we did, and as it turns out, carp aren't all that bad. Most of the country's aquatic ecosystems have adjusted to their presence and survived. There is even some commercial fishing for them. Carp flesh, it turns out, can be fashioned into croquettes that some people find edible, but no Southerner that I know has ever tried them.

After leaving Weston Lake, I follow the elevated boardwalk back into the forest, past pawpaw, dwarf palmetto, and ironwood, past huge sweet gums and towering oaks. Even among these giants, though, the loblolly pines stand out. There are not many of them in this predominately hardwood forest, and they do not occur in pure stands. In fact, they are usually separated from one another by long distances. Some of the loblollies between the lake and trailhead are among the tallest trees on the east coast, and one near the boardwalk is estimated to be 160 feet tall, about the height of a sixteen-story building. (The national champion loblolly pine in Arkansas is 188 feet tall.) My eyes follow the deeply fissured bark of the thick, straight trunk skyward to a canopy of dark-green needles.

The loblolly pine (*Pinus taeda*) is a common pine in the Southeast. It is fast growing and is the most important commercial tree in the region. Timber companies plant it in huge single-species stands to harvest for lumber or pulpwood. In the Carolinas, more acres of wilderness have been lost to pine monoculture than to all other forms of development, including farming. I've been through a loblolly farm and have seen row after dreary row of same-sized trees covering hundreds of acres. Though these farms are more environmentally friendly than, say, a Wal-Mart parking lot, they are visually and biologically boring because they lack the diversity of a natural forest. On the other hand, if the timber companies could meet their quotas by logging only loblolly farms, then their presence might help to protect our remaining wild forests. Unfortunately, that's not the way it works. Population growth demands an ever increasing supply of wood products. Unless that increase in demand can be met by higher yields per acre—which has so far not happened—the number of acres of loblolly pines planted in the South will continue to increase, and the number of acres of wild forest will continue to decrease.

Congaree Swamp, however, is protected against such encroachments, an outdoor museum for outlandishly sized loblollies, pines of a size you will never find on a tree farm. Some of these trees are three hundred years old, and all of them are anomalies, isolated evergreen sentinels in an otherwise 100 percent hardwood forest. Like all pines, loblollies need full sun to sprout and grow, conditions that exist in a hardwood forest only after a major disturbance, such as a hurricane or logging, has created gaps in the canopy. No one knows exactly what happened in these woods three hundred years ago that allowed these pines to take root and grow, but like the carp, another stranger in this swamp, they are doing quite well here.

At the end of the boardwalk, the swamp ends at a bluff that slopes up from the Congaree flood plain. I dip my finger in the rich swamp mud below the bluff. Did any of the millions of water molecules in the mud clinging to my finger start up on Sassafras Mountain and end up here, rather than in the Atlantic? The idea appeals to me, so I sniff the gooey stuff, and I swear I can smell—just for a second—a hint of tangy Appalachian air.

BEFORE YOU GO

For More Information

Congaree Swamp National Monument
200 Caroline Sims Road
Hopkins, S.C. 29061
(803) 776-4396

Accommodations

Congaree Swamp National Monument is only twenty miles southeast of Columbia, which offers a wide variety of hotels and motels. Contact

Columbia Metropolitan Visitor Center
1012 Gervais Street
Columbia, S.C. 29202
(800) 264-4884

Campgrounds

Primitive and backcountry camping are allowed in the national monument; a permit, which may be obtained for no charge at the ranger station, is required.

Maps

All of the trails are well marked, and the free trail map available at the ranger station is adequate for this walk.

Special Precautions

High water sometimes closes the monument's trails; check their condition with the park rangers before you go.

Additional Reading

The Alien Animals by George Laycock, The Natural History Press, New York, 1966.

Catesby's Birds of Colonial America edited by Alan Feduccia, The University of North Carolina Press, Chapel Hill, 1985. This book contains the complete text of Catesby's *The Natural History of Carolina, Florida, and the Bahama Islands*, which was originally published in London in 1731.

Life Histories of North American Woodpeckers by Arthur Cleveland Bent, Dover Publications, Inc., New York, 1964. This book was originally published in 1939 as Smithsonian Institution United States National Museum *Bulletin 174*.

"National Register of Big Trees: 1994 Edition" by Whit Bronaugh, *American Forests* 100, January/February 1994, 26-41.

South Carolina: The Making of a Landscape by Charles F. Kovacik and John J. Winberry, University of South Carolina Press, Columbia, 1988.

A SKYFUL OF BIRDS

Marshland Trail and Bike/Hike Trail
Santee Coastal Reserve

To reach the 24,000-acre Santee Coastal Reserve, take U.S. 17 south from Georgetown for about 15 miles. After crossing the South Santee River, go left on the first paved road, S.C. 857 (a small "Santee Coastal Reserve" sign marks this intersection). Follow it for 2.6 miles, then go left again on Santee Club Road, which leads into the reserve. The parking lot for the Marshland and Bike/Hike trails is on the right, a little less than 3 miles from the entrance.

From the parking lot, a broad track goes south to the Washo Reserve boardwalk, an 800-foot walkway leading to a black-water slough rimmed with bald cypresses and tupelo gums. From the boardwalk, the path continues south through a maritime forest and then turns east, where it intersects the Bike/Hike Trail. Follow the Bike/Hike Trail in a 5.7-mile counterclockwise loop through diked marshes that were once the growing fields of rice plantations. Return to trailhead on the northern leg of the Marshland Trail.

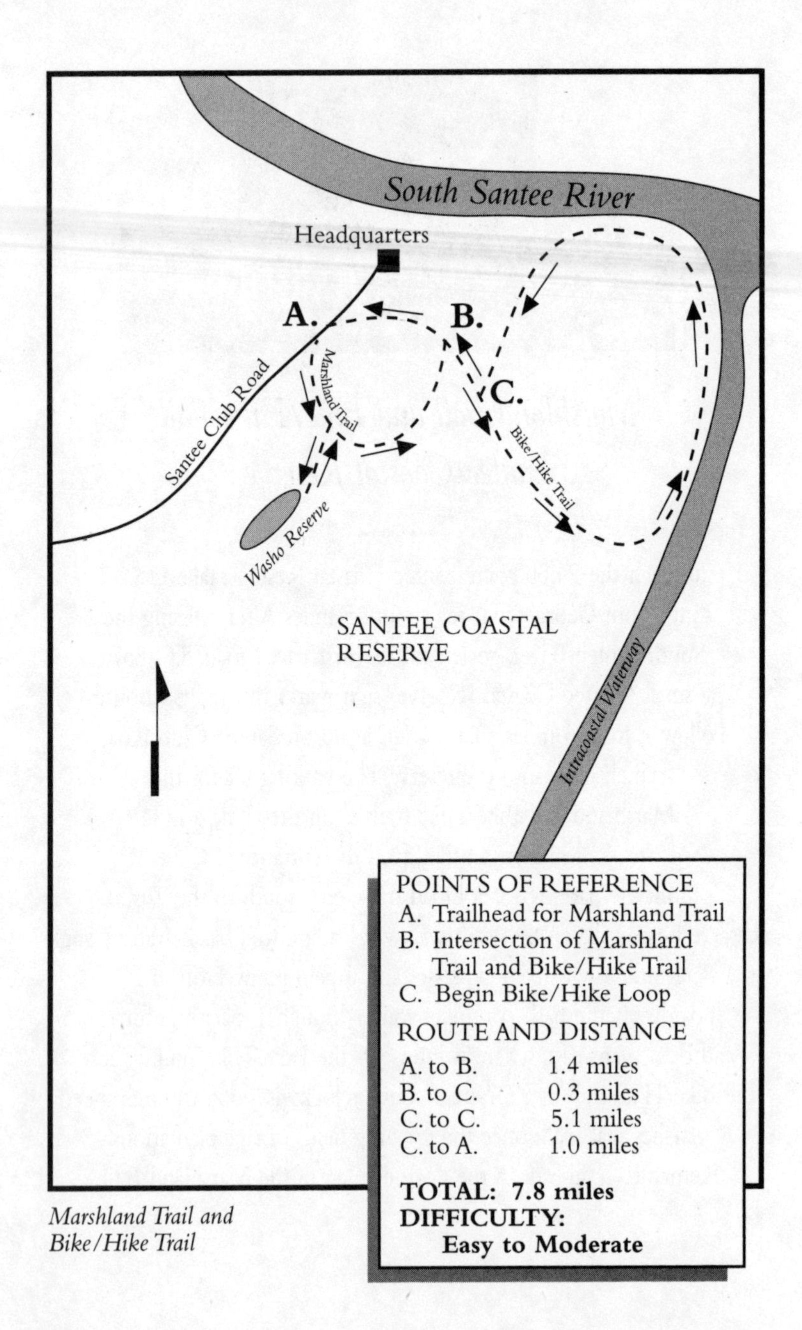

Marshland Trail and Bike/Hike Trail

A Skyful of Birds

The sandy road into Santee Coastal Reserve passes through a fine longleaf pine savanna, as open and airy as a suburban lawn. Less than three miles from the entrance, the Marshland Trail begins in the dense, dark-green tangle of a Carolina maritime forest of live oaks, wax myrtles, and loblolly pines. After several hundred yards of thick forest, the trail enters a cypress-tupelo gum swamp, damp and gray with Spanish moss. In just a few miles, a visitor to the reserve will have passed through three of the more important ecosystems found in South Carolina's coastal plain. But there is more. After another mile, the Marshland Trail curls north and intersects the Bike/Hike Trail, which leads southeast into the last and largest of the reserve's habitats—a watery expanse of impoundments and brackish-water marshes. Unlike the other ecosystems, the marshes are newcomers here, the remnants of a story that began just three hundred years ago.

Historians do not agree on the exact date that rice was introduced into South Carolina. They are certain, however, that by the beginning of the eighteenth century, it was an established crop in the low country.[1] The first rice was planted in the same way as corn or beans or any other crop. But some rice genius soon discovered that flooding the fields immediately after planting greatly increased yields. Unfortunately, the fields couldn't stay flooded; for the highest yields, they had to be periodically drained during the growing season, and for planting and harvesting. The problem of controlling water levels was solved by building a system of dikes and gates (called "trunks" in rice agriculture) along tidal rivers. The trunks were built at a point in the river where the water was still fresh, yet the water level was still affected by the tides. A field situated beside these trunks could be flooded with fresh water during high tides and drained during low tides.

Land meeting these specifications was not plentiful, and much of it was bought up by a few families. Over the years, these families fine-tuned rice-growing methods, and production grew. In 1765, 120,000 barrels of rice were shipped out of Charles Town, and rich rice planters roamed Meeting Street, looking

---

[1] See *River of the Carolinas: The Santee* by Henry Savage; *A South Carolina: Synoptic History for Laymen* by Lewis P. Jones; and *South Carolina: The Making of a Landscape* by Charles F. Kovacik and John J. Winberry.

for conversation or a horse race or a drink. The so-called "golden age" of the aristocrats of rice had arrived.

It didn't last long. Many planters had their fields destroyed and their plantation houses burned during the Revolutionary War. They slowly recovered, however, and rice—though supplanted by cotton as the state's most important agricultural crop—was still a significant part of South Carolina's economy until the Civil War. Rice is a labor-intensive crop, and the people who hacked down the trees and grubbed out the stumps in the swamps that originally covered the rice-growing part of the state were slaves. The people who built the dikes and dug the canals were slaves. And the people who planted the rice and harvested it in the sweltering September sun were slaves. In fact, the entire rice culture was built by the black muscle of unsalaried African labor. And the Civil War ended that.

After the war, low-country planters continued to grow rice, though in much smaller quantities, using freed slaves as laborers. The final blow didn't come until 1893, when a furious August hurricane wiped out the few planters still hanging on. Land prices, already low after the Civil War, dropped even further. Hunting clubs began acquiring thousands of acres of cheap, abandoned rice fields for the fine waterfowl shooting they provided. In 1974, one of them—the Santee Gun Club, which was founded in 1898—donated its property to the Nature Conservancy, which, in turn, deeded most of it to the state. The result was Santee Coastal Reserve, which is managed by the state's Wildlife and Marine Resources Department. The reserve's extensive system of dikes and trunks are vestiges of the old rice plantations—and an important legacy for migratory waterfowl.

Diane and I begin the Marshland Trail on a clear February morning. The weather is warm, and the air already smells of spring. A few fluffy cumulus clouds float in a deep-blue sky. Stormy weather, which keeps ducks flying, is best for duck hunting. But this is perfect weather for duck watching, since the birds should be settled down on the impoundments, where they are easier to study and identify.

The trail is wide and lined with six-foot-high yaupons and wax myrtles. Tall, slender loblolly pines and wide-spreading live oaks loom dark and green above the understory. The maritime forest quickly gives way to cypresses and tupelo gums and standing water. The trail leads to a boardwalk that passes over a cypress-studded slough and stops at large lake that is part of Washo Reserve, a 1,040-acre inholding owned by the Nature Conservancy.

The cypresses and gums that rim the lake are leafless at this time of year, so the color scheme is gray and black. Gray Spanish moss hangs from gray and black trees which are covered with splotches of gray lichens and surround a black-water lake. As we watch, the lake's center erupts; with a cacophony of quacks and whistles, twenty-five or so widgeons shoot into the air, trailed by a single great blue heron, whose long gray wings beat hard as it tries to keep up with the speedier ducks.

The stark colors of the swamp in winter suggest a total, if temporary, absence of photosynthetic life, but a closer look tells a different story. An inconspicuous green scum of duckweed and algae float near the shores of the lake. And though we can't see it, the bottom of the pond is almost certainly covered with grasses and pondweeds—favorite foods of ducks.

After the boardwalk, the trail reenters the maritime forest, passing dwarf palmettos, aromatic bays, evergreen hollies, and spindly red maples. Woodpeckers hammer away in the distance, and deer tracks crisscross the soft ground of the path. Near the trail, a huge live oak is riddled with sapsucker holes. A few down trees, and some still standing with their trunks snapped off, remind us that Hurricane Hugo sideswiped this area a few years ago. At a signed intersection, we turn southeast on the Bike/Hike Trail. The path leaves the cloistered, green forest and heads out into the blue skies and windy openness of the marsh. We are soon walking on a dike that is as straight and flat as a Kansas interstate.

Tall cordgrass (*Spartina cynosuroides*) lines both sides of the dike. Two grasslike plants, black needlerush (*Juncus roemerianus*) and saltmarsh bulrush (*Scirpus robustus*), grow in the shallow impoundments. To understand this marsh, however, one must not only observe what grows here, but also notice what is missing; saltmarsh cordgrass, *Spartina alterniflora*, the ubiquitous staple of nearly all southeastern salt marshes, is nowhere to be found.

In South Carolina, *S. alterniflora* is the dominant plant in low coastal marshes—marshes that are flooded by salt water at least once a day. The three most important plant species at Santee Reserve are usually found in the high marsh—marshes that are less frequently flooded by salt water. The impoundments here, however, the remains of old rice fields, are flooded most of the time. Why, then, should the plants of the high marsh dominate?

The answer lies in the salinity of the water. This is a brackish-water marsh, and *S. alterniflora*, which is superbly equipped to survive in the salty low marsh, cannot compete with species adapted to the milder conditions of the high marsh. Low-marsh plants can handle high concentrations of salt, while high-marsh and brackish-water marsh plants are better equipped for less saline conditions, and it is the salinity that determines which plants thrive. A brackish-water marsh, even if it is regularly (or almost continuously) flooded, more closely resembles the drier high marsh in salinity than it does the wetter, but saltier, low marsh.

A north wind whips across the impoundments, causing the hollow stems of the brown, ten-foot-tall cordgrass growing beside the dike to rattle and squeak like hundreds of baby birds crying for food. A red-tailed hawk rides the wind above the marsh, and two huge birds, which might be bald eagles, sail over the pine trees on the horizon. The quietness of the morning is shattered by a commotion of squawking and splashing in the impoundment to our right. Near the center of the impoundment, a hundred or so dark shapes mill about on the water.

Santee Reserve is operated—farmed, in fact—to attract migratory waterfowl. The reserve's managers raise and lower the trunks along the dikes, adjusting the salinity and the depth of the impoundments, to provide optimum growing conditions for dwarf spike rush, widgeon grass, and sago pondweed—foods favored by dabbling ducks—much as the old rice planters adjusted water levels to maximize yields of their crop. This year the reserve has been spectacularly successful. Tommy Strange, Santee's manager, told us before we began our walk that over fifty thousand ducks—mallards, teal, and pintails; widgeons, gadwalls, and shovelers—were wintering at the refuge this season. But aside from the small flock at Washo Reserve, we haven't seen any of them until now. With my binoculars, I study the birds on the impoundment. They are several hundred yards away and hard to make out, a raft of indeterminate black bodies. Finally, I see something I can identify: white bills flashing in the sun. Tommy obviously omitted one other species attracted to the refuge, one that the members of the Santee Gun Club would almost certainly not approve. These birds are unmistakably . . . coots.

The American coot (*Fulica americana*) is not well thought of by duck hunters. In the first place, coots aren't ducks at all but members of the family Rallidae (or rail family), a group of birds described in my field guide as "ducklike." And duck hunters, who, like fly fishermen, tend to be purists, scorn off-breeds like rails. Coots are supposed to taste bad, too, which is another strike against them as far as duck hunters are concerned. Finally, there is the matter of names. Coots are also known as mud hens, crow bills, and, for reasons unknown to me, blue peters. And no self-respecting duck hunter could ever announce to his friends that he is going "blue-peter hunting."

As we walk, shimmering flocks of green-and-white tree swallows swoop and swerve over the impoundments, snatching unseen insects from the air. A dozen red-winged blackbirds flutter in the dust on the path ahead, and twenty or thirty coots skitter along the top of the water, keeping a safe distance in front of us. Then, three pelicans cruise by, heading toward the sea. Far out on the impoundment, a huge flock of dark specks takes off from the water and flies away from the reserve—ducks heading north.

At the end of the cross-impoundment dike, the trail turns north and parallels the Intracoastal Waterway. After a few steps, a loud splash startles us as a five-foot alligator scrambles off the bank and vanishes into a canal. Water lilies and cattails grow in the canal, so the water flowing in it must be fresh, or close to it—a requirement for gators.

The trail then passes through a wax myrtle thicket. A few pines occupy the higher ground, but most of them are dead, victims of Hugo. A snowy egret poses on one of the bleached snags. A few sugarberries and cedars grow beside the path, and a gallinule tiptoes through the marsh grass on the far side of the canal. Because of its varied ecosystems, Santee Reserve is richer in wildlife and plants and trees than most natural areas. But where, I wonder, is the main attraction? Where are the ducks? I know they are here; we've seen black dots on the impoundments and in the sky, but they were too far away to identify as more than generic ducks. Unfortunately, I'm beginning to suspect that's as close as we are going to get to the big flocks today.

The birds are rightfully wary. Even though public duck hunting is prohibited at the reserve, duck blinds are scattered through the impoundments, and we've already passed several piles of bright-yellow shotgun shells on the dikes. It turns out that when the state acquired the property, the Santee Gun Club retained—for a handsome price—the right to continue limited waterfowl hunting on reserve lands.

The agreement seems to be fair. After rice planting ended here, the dikes would have soon fallen into disrepair and crumbled. The gun club maintained them for many years at their own expense and kept the property intact for waterfowl. True, their motives were not entirely pure; they wanted good hunting. But thanks to them, the dikes are still here, now on property open to the public for most of the year, and so are the ducks—even if it's hard to get close enough to identify them.

At the easternmost point of the reserve, the trail veers northwest and parallels the South Santee River on yet another dike. Diane asks how I, the principal bird watcher in our family, can spend most of a day among these impoundments and miss fifty thousand ducks. She then asks, for the third time, how many species I have identified today and grins evilly when I raise a single finger.

There's plenty of other wildlife, though, and as we walk, we continue to flush one thing or another—gators and coots, gallinules and herons, egrets and an occasional gull. Finally, three ducks burst from the water close enough for me to get a good look at them. They are mallards, and their noisy exit does not go unnoticed.

A second later, the entire impoundment explodes with ducks. A swarm of swallows and a batch of red-winged blackbirds quickly join the confusion, and for one magic moment the sky is literally filled with flashing wings and scolding calls. Some of the ducks are close enough to identify, but I am so entranced by the scene that I fail to focus on a single bird long enough to do so. I have no idea how many birds we saw in that moment, no idea of how many it takes to fill the sky. It was probably only a tiny fraction of the ducks wintering here, but for the first time, I begin to grasp the reality behind the number *fifty thousand*.

After the birds scatter and the sky clears, I turn to Diane and hold up two fingers. She laughs, and we continue down the dike. Bleached crab carapaces litter the path, and egrets stand like whitewashed statues in the marshes on the far side of the river. The trail turns north, and we plunge back into the maritime forest for the last leg of the walk. A common sulfur butterfly, perhaps a little groggy this early in the year, flies erratically around us and lights on a nearby yaupon bush. The butterfly, considerably less cautious than the reserve's skittish ducks, moves to Diane's extended finger and finally perches on my ear. It's a tickling, curious bug, and it crawls around my ear until we start walking again, then flaps off to another yaupon.

Back at the car, we grab water bottles and stroll over to the large, well-tended yard in front of the Santee Gun Club's clubhouse. While Diane snaps pictures, I sit on the grass and lean back against a sprawling moss-draped live oak. I close my eyes and remember the birds—a wondrous skyful of birds.

BEFORE YOU GO

For More Information

Santee Coastal Reserve
P.O. Box 37
McClellanville, S.C. 29458
(803) 546-8665

Accommodations

The nearest motels are in Georgetown, fifteen miles north of the reserve. Contact

Georgetown Visitor Center
162 Broad Street
Georgetown, S.C. 29440
(803) 546-8437

Campgrounds

Primitive camping is allowed in the reserve from February 1 to November 1. A written permit, which may be picked up for no charge at the reserve office, is required.

The closest developed campgrounds are in Francis Marion National Forest. For information, contact

Francis Marion National Forest
1835 Assembly Street
Strom Thurmond Building
Columbia, S.C. 29202
(803) 765-5222

Maps

The free trail map entitled "Santee Coastal Reserve Management Area" is excellent and suitable for this walk.

Special Precautions

During the warm months, mosquitoes and deer flies are as thick—and as fierce—here as any place I have ever been. I once visited the reserve in early May, and even when slathered with repellent, I guessed that my lifespan in the maritime forest would have been five minutes or less. Santee Reserve is one of South Carolina's greatest treasures, but it is one best enjoyed in cold weather.

Special Requirements

Santee Coastal Reserve is closed to the public from November 1 to February 1 and is open only in the afternoons during the month of February. Special visits are allowed during those months with the permission of the reserve's manager.

Additional Reading

Field Guide to Coastal Wetlands Plants of the Southeastern United States by Ralph W. Tiner, The University of Massachusetts Press, Amherst, 1993. This is an excellent guide to the plants of the southeastern marshes and a welcome addition to the libraries of Southern naturalists.

Life and Death of the Salt Marsh by John and Mildred Teal, Ballantine Books, New York, 1969. Although primarily focused on the marshes of the northeast, this classic book tells a great deal about the inner workings of a salt marsh.

River of the Carolinas: The Santee by Henry Savage, Jr., The University of North Carolina Press, Chapel Hill, 1956.

South Carolina: A Synoptic History for Laymen by Lewis P. Jones, Sandlapper Publishing, Inc., Orangeburg, South Carolina, 1971.

South Carolina Bird Life by Alexander Sprunt, Jr., and E. Burnham Chamberlain, University of South Carolina Press, Columbia, 1949.

South Carolina: The Making of a Landscape by Charles F. Kovacik and John J. Winberry, University of South Carolina Press, Columbia, 1988.

METAMORPHOSIS IN GREEN

Swamp Fox Trail
Francis Marion National Forest

The southern trailhead of the Swamp Fox Trail is just off U.S. 17, near the town of Awendaw, about 10 miles southwest of McClellanville. A sign on U.S. 17 marks the entrance to the parking lot.

From its southern terminus, the Swamp Fox Trail heads northwest into the 250,000-acre Francis Marion National Forest for 20.8 miles and ends near the town of Huger. Unfortunately, the last 9 miles of the trail were badly damaged by Hurricane Hugo and were still closed in 1994. This in-and-out walk is on the southernmost 3.5 miles of the trail. It passes through enough country to give the hiker a sense of the diversity and resilience of this coastal forest, as it recovers from Hugo.

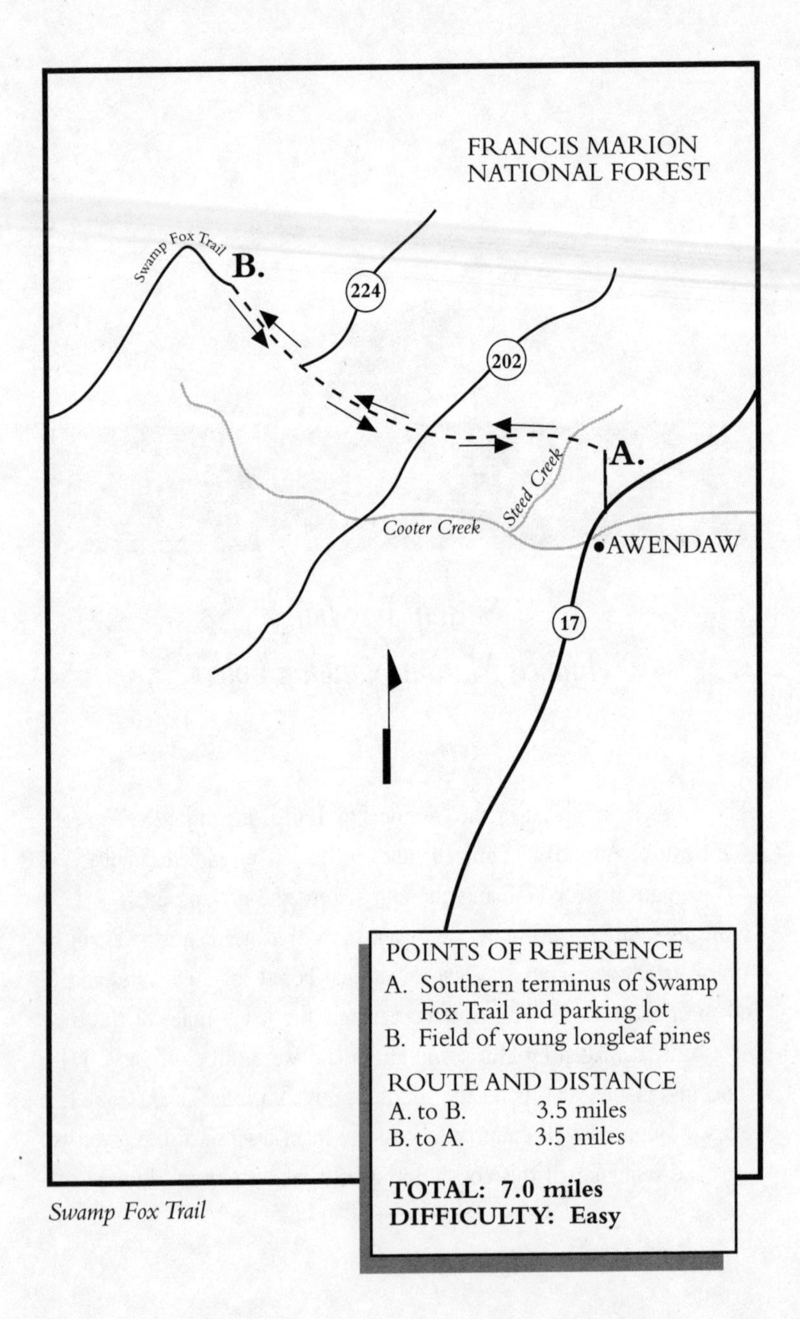

Swamp Fox Trail

Metamorphosis in Green

Diane and I start the Swamp Fox Trail in Francis Marion National Forest on a warm, overcast day in early May. The names of both the forest and the trail honor Francis Marion, one of South Carolina's greatest Revolutionary War heroes. And having just finished Robert Bass's biography of him, both the man and metamorphosis are on my mind. The two are connected for me because of a goofy episode in Marion's life.

On March 19, 1780—well before his heroics earned him the sobriquet of "Swamp Fox"—Lieutenant Colonel Francis

Marion attended a private dinner party in Charleston. At the time, many South Carolinians were Tory supporters, loyal to the British crown, but the partygoers at the house on Tradd Street that night were Whigs. After dinner, the host locked the doors and the group began toasting life, liberty, and the Whig cause with "bumpers of sparkling wine." Marion, whom Bass describes as a moody, scrawny, deeply religious Huguenot, stayed sober and, tiring of the party, left by jumping out of a second-story window, breaking his ankle when he landed.

Now, I can understand why Francis Marion wanted to leave the party; it's no fun being sober among a bunch of drinkers—even if they are Whigs. But why didn't he just ask the host to let him out the front door? Or if, for some reason, that seemed dangerous, why didn't he sneak out the back door or jump out a *first-story* window? It's possible the Swamp Fox would have good answers to these questions. But it's just as likely that he had, as most of us do occasionally, a boneheaded moment, a flash of pure *dumbness*. I have broken a few of my own bones, and I'd hate to try to explain those accidents—especially the one involving the rented motorcycle.

Three weeks later, as Charleston was about to fall to the British, Francis Marion—unable to walk—escaped the town, crossing the Cooper River on a litter and disappearing into the Santee swamps. Within a few years, the man who broke his ankle by jumping out of a window had transformed himself into the wily Swamp Fox, a brilliant military tactician who successfully harassed the British over much of eastern South Carolina.

The trail begins among a cluster of vine-hung sweet gums no more than twenty feet tall. Purple asters and wisteria grow near the trail. The cloying smell of honeysuckle is heavy in the air.

Less than five years ago, Hurricane Hugo slammed into the coast just a few miles southeast of here, and though the countryside is verdurous and healthy, it is mostly chest-high brush. All that's left of the forest that once grew here are a few isolated trees and numerous bleached snags with their tops snapped off. What used to be shady forest floor is now exposed to sunlight, allowing switch cane, wildflowers, and ferns to flourish. Small red maples and water oaks and wax myrtles barely rise above the understory. The large white flowers of sweet bays peek out from dense, shiny-green leaves, making that tree easy to distinguish from the similar-leaved red bay, which produces a tiny yellow flower.

Near the trail, a chainsaw artist has carved a chair from the remains of a tree. The chair, still attached to the stump, is rough cut but perfectly formed. After Hugo, a lot of people passed this way with chain saws to clear the trail, and at least one of them must have had a whimsical, creative streak. I look for the artist's name or initials but find nothing.

A wooden bridge leads over a clear, three-foot-wide stream. The low *catung, catung, catung* of green frogs comes from the creek, and bright flowers of orange milkwort appear among the ferns near the path. I spot a patch of netted chain ferns, but the most plentiful species here is the Christmas fern.

The Christmas fern (*Polystichum acrostichoides*) grows in all regions of South Carolina, and it is probably the most abundant fern in the eastern United States. Its broad evergreen fronds, with leaflets shaped like Christmas stockings, make it one of the easier members of this group to identify.

Like the liverworts and mosses, ferns are primitive plants. They are hard to identify because they do not produce flowers, the most important features in the classification and identification of modern plants. Without flowers, ferns have had to develop a complicated sex life, involving both sexual and asexual generation. Books about ferns usually depict this life cycle as an elaborate circular diagram that I suspect only ferns can understand. For the rest of us, it is important only to know that the cycle starts with a single-celled reproductive unit called a spore.

Spores are found on the back of some fronds in tiny cases called *sori*. The arrangement of sori on a frond helps naturalists identify the fern, much as the blooms on a wildflower help to identify it. Unfortunately, most fronds are sterile and have no sori. So the first step in identifying a fern by this method is to find a fertile frond.

I examine the plant nearest me, flipping over fronds and checking the underside of each one. No sori. I look at more fronds. Same result. Finally, I pinch off a leaflet. It does indeed look just like a stocking. "Christmas fern," I say into my tape recorder. "Sterile Christmas fern."

The trail continues northwest beyond the creek. We cross a dirt road, then come to another creek, wide and clear, but dark with tannin. An iridescent blue dragonfly hunts among small red maples near the water, and several sizable cypresses grow along the banks. Small crowns, buttressed trunks, and knee-anchored root systems supposedly give cypresses a better chance of surviving a hurricane than pines or hardwoods, a supposition upheld by the presence of these trees.

Beyond the creek, the path is lined with blackberries and thistles. The brush is relieved only by an occasional tree or snag. The trail parallels an old cattail-choked canal, and the calls of frogs come from every direction, loud and constant. Mounds of dirt lie in sunny spots beside the trail. When I scrape the top off one, thousands of tiny red ants come boiling out, ready for battle.

The trail crosses another road and enters a patch of woods thick with oaks and maples and loblolly pines. It's as if Hugo decided to leave a remnant of forest to remind us of how this land once looked. But it's only a small patch, and the country quickly opens up again. Small bays and sassafras trees, hardly more than bushes, line the path, and fifteen-foot-tall swamp chestnut oaks, tulip poplars, and a smattering of pines take advantage of the full sun. So do butterflies of several sizes and colors.

Among the orange-and-black viceroys and red-spotted purples, floats a lazy giant, a bat-sized butterfly with brown wings, marked with yellow and blue spots. It flies down the path in front of us, stopping to perch about every twenty feet, then flying on. Its size makes it easy to identify; this is a palamedes swallowtail, a butterfly of the great southern swamps.

The wingspan of the palamedes swallowtail (*Pterourus palamedes*) can exceed five inches, though this one is smaller. The species occurs along the Atlantic and Gulf coasts from Maryland to Mexico, but it seems to do best in swamps. Though they prefer wetter terrain, it is not surprising to find these swallowtails in the dry, open country near the trail; their caterpillars feed almost exclusively on red bay, sweet bay, and sassafras, which are abundant here, and the adults sip nectar from thistles, which are also plentiful.

Some nature writers have called the life cycle of the butterflies "the incredible miracle of metamorphosis." I have seen pictures of the ugly, green caterpillars from which the huge, colorful palamedes swallowtails are manufactured, and "miracle" may not be too strong a word for the change. And it seems especially fitting to find this wonderfully transformed creature here on the Swamp Fox Trail in Francis Marion's forest.

The trail climbs imperceptibly north and west, but the changes in landscape are noticeable. Young longleaf pines grow in the ragged underbrush of snag-studded fields, and their numbers increase as the land becomes drier and sandier. A welcome breeze blows in from the south, and a bobwhite calls softly in the distance. A red-headed woodpecker, a striking mosaic of blacks and whites and red, works a dead pine no more than thirty feet from the path.

The trail then enters a larger field, and there in front of us is the future—thousands of chest-high longleaf pines. The property that became Francis Marion National Forest was a farmed-out, logged-out mess when the forest service took it over in 1936. But before unsound agricultural and logging practices degraded the land, foresters believe that much of it was covered by a longleaf-pine savanna, and the field of pines in front of us suggests that, in time, some of the land will revert to it again. We find a log to sit on. Chickadees flutter about in the underbrush, and a great crested flycatcher flies to a nearby snag. Before Hugo, red-cockaded woodpeckers, which do best in old-growth pine forests, were numerous here, but only one-third of the population survived the hurricane. And though their numbers have bounced back, we have not seen one today. I pick out a few turkey oaks and red oaks among the pines. They remind me that another ingredient besides time is needed for this forest to fulfill its destiny; periodic fires will be required to keep the oaks from supplanting the pines.[1]

Recurrent fires, caused by lightning strikes or Indians in pre-European pine forests, are necessary to maintain a longleaf-pine savanna. Since wildfires are too dangerous these days, they are suppressed and foresters use deliberately set controlled burns in their place. Because of the numerous roads and inholdings in Francis Marion National Forest, those burns present a problem for foresters. Motorists and landowners tend to get irate when smoke blows across their highways and property. This is a critical issue for the forest service, since they want and need public support to carry out their mission–which includes re-creating a longleaf-pine savanna here.

A new forest-management plan is expected to be completed in 1995. The plan will almost certainly be a compromise, an attempt to balance the needs of the timber industry, the red-cockaded woodpecker, and the recreational user with the forest service's overall responsibility for ecosystem management. But

---

[1] See "A Winter's Walk" (pages 121–134) for a fuller explanation of the role fires play in the longleaf pine-wire grass ecosystem.

nature has a say, too, and with the slightest encouragement, sixty or seventy years will surely transmute this field of scrawny saplings into a shady forest of tall longleaf pines.

After our rest, we begin the walk back. Katydids click hoarsely in the tall brown grasses bordering the path, and trumpet honeysuckle climbs over the bushes. A kingbird sits atop a snag, and towhees scratch industriously in the dead leaves beneath blackberry bushes. Although it is still overcast, the temperature has passed the line that separates warm from hot. Sweat drips from my nose, and my feet feel heavy. The gray clouds shading the sun darken further, and the smell of rain is in the air. Diane stops suddenly and points toward the sky. "What are *those*?" she asks.

I stop to look. Two elegant birds float effortlessly overhead, and though I have never seen one before, their name rolls off my tongue as if I had been waiting for them to appear. "Swallow-tailed kites," I say reverently. "It's a pair of swallow-tailed kites."

Every description of swallow-tailed kites (*Elanoides forficatus*) that I have read—from Audubon's to Roger Tory Peterson's—has the word "grace" or "graceful" in it. One glance at the birds above us tells me why. They are mostly white, about the size of a herring gull. Their long pointed wings and deeply forked tails are delicately edged in black. These birds hang like silhouettes in the sky, defying gravity seemingly without exertion. Like their man-made namesakes, swallow-tailed kites are perfectly designed airfoils, an important feature for birds that eat and drink in flight and return to earth only to roost and nest. They prey principally on insects, which they catch in the air, and on small reptiles, which they pluck from the ground and then eat in the air. They drink by skimming the surface of ponds, gulping water as they fly.

E. forficatus once nested as far north as Minnesota, but by 1938, they were rarely seen outside of Florida. Today, their range appears to be expanding. Though swallow-tailed kites are still much more abundant in Florida than in any other state, they are also found in parts of four other southern states. Our sighting may help confirm this welcome enlargement of their range; according to the map in my field guide, these kites aren't supposed to occur this far north in South Carolina.

As we watch, the birds soar ever higher, never once flapping a wing. Finally, they are mere white specks in the dark sky, but we continue to watch until they are no longer visible.

Seeing the kites has transformed our day, and though the weather is unchanged, the sky seems brighter, and we trot down the trail in high spirits. By the time we get back to trailhead, the sun is dimly visible through the clouds, and the threat of rain has passed.

Though Hugo dramatically altered the landscape along the Swamp Fox Trail, there is a timelessness, a stability about this country that intrigues and delights. The lush ferns and blackwater creeks and great brown butterflies will still be here when the longleaf saplings have grown and changed field back to forest, when the tall cypresses and hardwoods are once again thick along the creeks and in the bottomlands.

Francis Marion, whose final home was northeast of here near the Santee River, loved this country, too, loved hunting and fishing and farming here. But fighting in it for so many years ruined his health, and he was only sixty-three years old when he died in 1795. After his death, Robert Bass says that eulogists attempted to remake the real man—the moody little Huguenot with a talent for soldiering—into a legend, a Revolutionary War Robin Hood. But Marion's deeds need no exaggeration; he was a true hero whose courage affected the outcome of the Revolutionary War—which is why the Tradd Street episode is so fascinating. It shows the Swamp Fox as he started out, an ordinary man subject to making the same blunders as the rest of us. But he was a man who was resilient enough to transform himself in troubled times. And it is apt that the forest and trail named for him appear to have that same resilience.

BEFORE YOU GO

For More Information

Francis Marion National Forest is made up of two ranger districts. The southeastern section of the Swamp Fox Trail, the part covered in this chapter, is in the Wambaw district; the northwestern part of the trail is in the Witherbee district.

Wambaw Ranger District
Francis Marion National Forest
P.O. Box 788
McClellanville, S.C. 29458
(803) 887-3257

Witherbee Ranger District
HC 69, Box 1532
Moncks Corner, S.C. 29461
(803) 336-3248

Accommodations

The nearest towns with hotels and motels are Mount Pleasant (just north of Charleston), Georgetown, and Moncks Corner. Contact

Charleston Convention and Visitors Bureau
P.O. Box 975
Charleston, S.C. 29402
(803) 577-2510

Georgetown Visitor Center
162 Broad Street
Georgetown, S.C. 29440
(803) 546-8437

Berkeley County Chamber of Commerce
P.O. Box 905
Moncks Corner, S.C. 29461
(803) 761-8238

Campgrounds

Francis Marion National Forest has five developed campgrounds. For information, contact either of the ranger districts at the addresses given above. There are also primitive campsites for backpackers hiking the Swamp Fox Trail at Halfway Creek Trail Camp.

Maps

The map in the free forest service brochure "Guide to the Swamp Fox Trail" is adequate for this walk.

Special Precautions

Deer hunting is popular here. Only part of the national forest is open to hunting, but one should avoid those areas during the fall hunting season, except on Sundays when hunting is prohibited. A special map issued by the forest service specifies which areas are open to hunting, and when.

Unlike hunting, ticks and mosquitoes are rarely out of season at Francis Marion. You might get by without bug repellent in midwinter, but the safest course is to take some with you at all times.

Additional Reading

Ferns of the Coastal Plain: Their Lore, Legends and Uses by Lin Dunbar, University of South Carolina Press, Columbia, 1989.

Life Histories of North American Birds of Prey: Part 1 by Arthur Cleveland Bent, Dover Publications, New York, 1961. This book was originally published in 1937 as Smithsonian Institution United States National Museum *Bulletin 167*.

The Lives of the Butterflies by Matthew M. Douglas, The University of Michigan Press, Ann Arbor, 1986.

Swamp Fox: The Life and Campaigns of General Francis Marion by Robert D. Bass, Sandlapper Publishing Co., Inc., Orangeburg, South Carolina, 1974. This book was first published in 1959 by Henry Holt and Company.

"An Up & Coming Forest" by Virginia Beach, *South Carolina Wildlife* 40, January/February, 1993, 44-49. This is an excellent article about the condition of Francis Marion National Forest after Hurricane Hugo and the National Forest Service's plans to re-create the longleaf-pine ecosystem.

A WINTER'S WALK

Tate's Trail
Carolina Sandhills National Wildlife Refuge

The headquarters of the 45,000-acre Carolina Sandhills National Wildlife Refuge is 4 miles north of McBee on U.S. 1. Tate's Trail begins at the Lake Bee Recreation Area, about 6 miles north of U.S. 1 on S.C. 145.

From the Lake Bee parking lot, Tate's Trail runs southeast to Martins Lake and stops at an observation tower at the far end of the lake. The return to trailhead is by the same route.

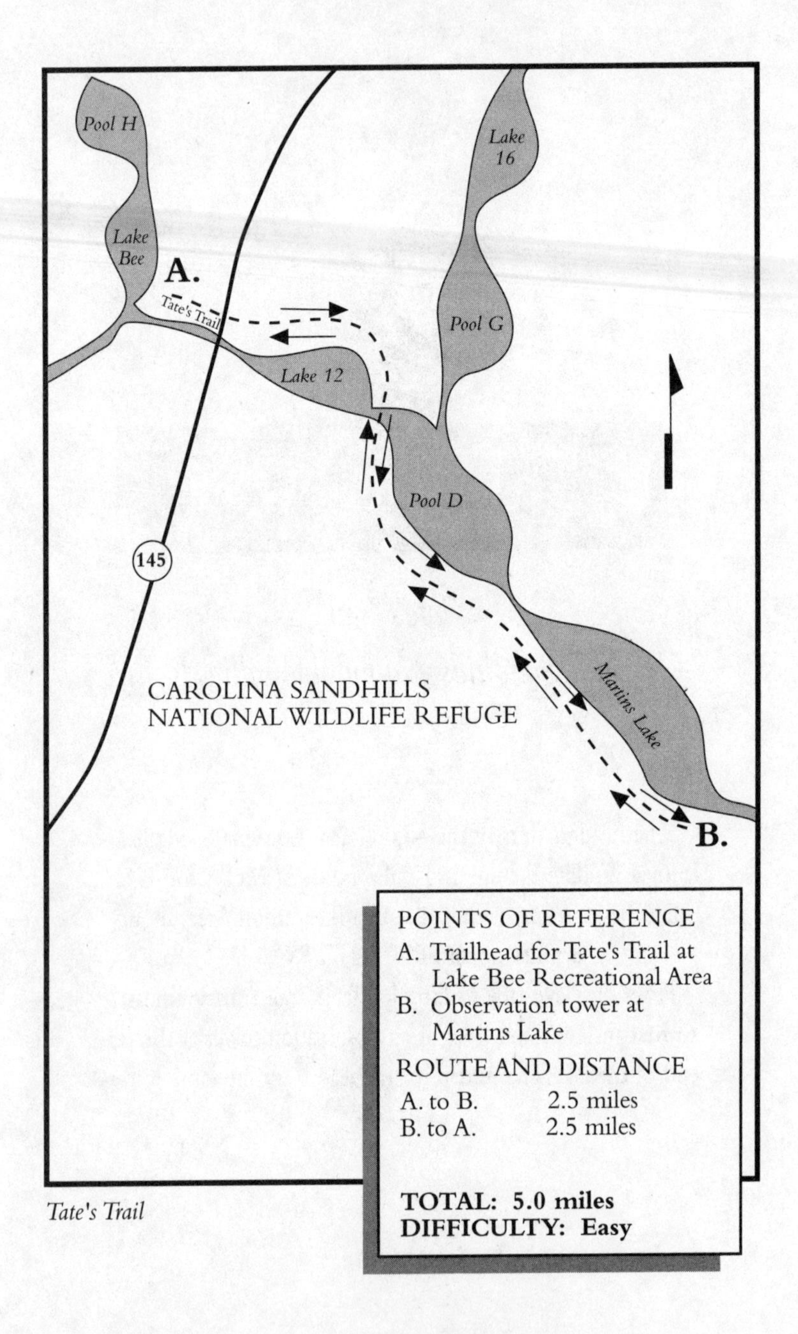
Pool H
Lake Bee
A.
Tate's Trail
Lake 16
Pool G
Lake 12
Pool D
145
Martins Lake
B.
CAROLINA SANDHILLS
NATIONAL WILDLIFE REFUGE
POINTS OF REFERENCE
A. Trailhead for Tate's Trail at Lake Bee Recreational Area
B. Observation tower at Martins Lake
ROUTE AND DISTANCE
A. to B. 2.5 miles
B. to A. 2.5 miles
TOTAL: 5.0 miles
DIFFICULTY: Easy

Tate's Trail

A Winter's Walk

When I needed an outing to rid myself of the cabin fever that often afflicts me in January, I decided to revisit Carolina Sandhills National Wildlife Refuge. The refuge had been a favorite of mine years ago when we lived near it, and I still consider it an old friend and teacher, a place that offered lessons I am still trying to absorb. I didn't decide to go there because January is its best month; in fact, only a few ducks and geese winter at the refuge these days, and the place is much prettier in the warmer months, when its astonishing array of wildflowers are in bloom.

No, I chose it for a winter's walk because I had never been there in that season and because I wanted to see what I could learn from it in the middle of what Shakespeare called our "three crabbed months."

As its name implies, the refuge is located in the state's sandhills region, the innermost part of the coastal plain. The sandhills are remnants of an ancient estuary formed when Piedmont rivers dumped huge loads of sand and silt into the ocean, which at the time covered the coastal plain. When sea levels dropped and the ocean retreated, an ecosystem formed on the sand dunes—the longleaf pine and wire grass savanna, which in pre-European times covered sixty million acres of the South.

European settlers consumed almost every tree on almost every one of those sixty million acres. The pines were tapped for their resin to make tar and pitch and turpentine, and they were cut down for lumber. Before the nineteenth century ended, the longleaf pine forest that had covered the land we now call Carolina Sandhills National Wildlife Refuge was gone.

The residents of the area turned to farming. But these are the *sand*hills, and it's hard to scratch out a living from ground where the soil is mostly sand. By the time the government started acquiring property there in the mid-1930s, most of the farmers had given up, leaving behind them land that was heavily eroded and, as one report put it, "essentially a biological desert." It wasn't until the refuge was created in 1939, that the land, assisted by the men and women who worked there, began to heal.

The United States Fish and Wildlife Service, with the help of the Civilian Conservation Corps, built picnic shelters for people and thirty small impoundments for waterfowl. And, of course, they planted pines, first in the 1930s and 1940s, then later in the 1960s. Today, longleaf pines blanket the rolling hills, but no matter how hard or how smart you work, restoring nature takes time. And though the reborn ecosystem that prevails on the refuge today is healthy, it is not identical to the one that existed in pre-European times—as we shall see on our walk.

From the Lake Bee Recreation Area, Diane and I start Tate's Trail on a cool, gray day. Immediately after leaving the recreation area, the trail crosses S.C. 145 and enters the forest. The air smells of rain, and damp oak leaves muffle the sound of our footsteps. A few patches of spiky, yellowish wire grass hug the ground, and bare turkey oaks and blackjack oaks grow beneath tall longleaf pines. The bark on almost every tree is charred to shoulder height, the result of controlled burns started by refuge personnel. Once, lightning or Indians set the fires, but uncontrolled wildfires are too dangerous these days, so the men and women who run the refuge must start—and control—the fires.

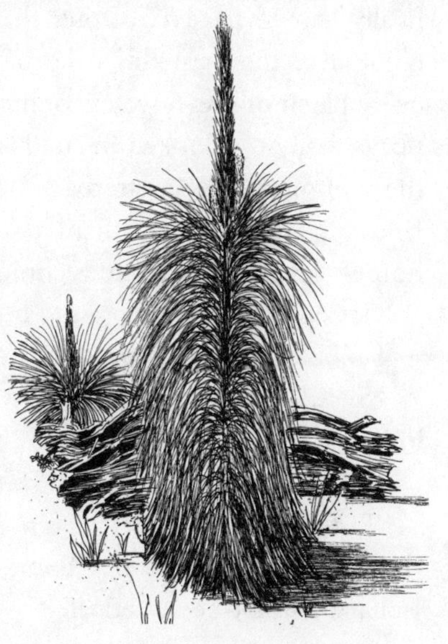

The refuge began controlled burning in the early 1960s when ecologists realized that a self-sustaining longleaf pine forest could not exist without fire. Surface fires—fires which burn the understory but do not reach the crowns of mature pines—kill the oaks, which shade the forest floor and prevent new pines from sprouting, but do little damage to the thick-barked, fire-resistant pines. With fewer oaks, the longleaf seedlings can soak up sunlight from gaps in the canopy created when older pines die and fall. The result, once the oaks are gone, is a nearly pure stand of longleaf pines, with a wire grass understory—the forest that existed before Europeans settled here.

But turkey oaks are tough, and those along Tate's Trail show that Carolina Sandhills still has a way to go before its pine forests are 100 percent self-sustaining. Ricky Ingram, the refuge manager, is well aware of the situation; he told us before we started our walk that he expects to have to burn up to fifteen thousand acres a year for several more years in order to thin out the oaks in the understory. And even after he gets the refuge the way he wants it, he will still need to burn five thousand acres a year to maintain it.

The trail heads southeast, along the north shore of the romantically named Lake 12. Other than the pines, there's not a lot of color near the path this time of year, so we stop to check out every patch of green we encounter, mostly shrubs and small trees, plants easily overlooked in the lushness of summer. We recognize the common ones—fetterbush and gallberry, titi and sweet bay. But some of them are hard to identify, and Diane tries some home-grown, unscientific techniques to figure them out.

"Taste this," she says, passing me a three-inch-long elliptic leaf.

I nibble on it. "Sweet, very sweet."

"Sure," she says. "It's called sweetleaf or horse sugar. Horses love it."

I peek at my field guide. "*Symplocos tinctoria*?"

"I guess."

"Ha! According to my book, sweetleaf is deciduous. This is January, it can't be sweetleaf."

"You have a better idea?"

I search through the field guide, then take another bite of leaf. "Sweetleaf," I say into my recorder. "Screwed-up sweetleaf."

The trail crosses to the south side of Lake 12 by way of a dam and continues southeast. Switch cane and red maples and loblolly pines grow along the creek below the dam, and the constant hammering of woodpeckers follows us. The red-cockaded woodpecker (*Picoides borealis*) lives among the pines on this refuge. It is an endangered species, so dependent on old-growth forests that it is sometimes referred to as the South's spotted owl. Years ago, I spotted my first red-cockaded woodpecker here, and I hope to see one today. Carolina Sandhills is a good place to look for these uncommon woodpeckers; it has more of them than all the other wildlife refuges combined. Though many more red-cockaded woodpeckers live in other state and national forests, this refuge is clearly important in the fight to save the species.

The red-cockaded woodpecker drills its nesting cavities exclusively in pines. But unlike other woodpeckers, it invariably selects living trees, usually mature pines sixty or more years old. Drilling a nesting cavity in a live pine is hard work, and it can take a woodpecker a year or more to finish one. Biologists believe that red-cockaded woodpeckers choose older trees because they are more likely to be infected with red heart, a disease that softens the non-living heartwood in the center of the tree and eases the labor of excavation.

Red-cockaded woodpeckers also forage for food on pines. In this, too, they prefer older trees. In young pines, the bark clings tightly to the trunk, but on mature trees, it forms large, loose plates. The red-cockaded woodpecker is adept at knocking the plates off those trees and helping themselves to the spiders and insects they uncover. Their highly specialized feeding and nesting requirements have made it hard for these woodpeckers to adapt to losses of habitat, and the decline of the species correlates directly to the disappearance of the great Southern pine forests.

Tate's Trail climbs up, away from the lake. Lichen-covered hickories and oaks line both sides of the path. Beneath them are leafless blueberry bushes, whose canes have turned green in a last-gasp effort at winter photosynthesis. Deer tracks dimple the sandy trail, and a pile of white feathers and bleached bones lie beside the dark trunk of an oak. We cross a tiny, clear, fast-flowing creek. It is getting colder and darker, but so far no rain.

The trail passes Pool D. I don't know who names the bodies of water on wildlife refuges, but I imagine a stone-faced, khaki-clad Jack Webb type with a severe alphanumeric fixation going from refuge to refuge, reminding the managers to "Just stick to the facts." Pool D is full of stumps and covered with aquatic vegetation. It appears to be perfect waterfowl habitat, but there are no ducks or geese on the lake.

Carolina Sandhills was never as popular with waterfowl as the coastal refuges, but over seven thousand ducks and geese wintered here in the early 1970s. This year, the number is down to five hundred or less. And though the loss of some northern breeding grounds has reduced their totals in the last twenty-five years, large numbers of ducks and geese still ply the Atlantic flyway.

So why the precipitous drop at Carolina Sandhills? Unlike the decline of the red-cockaded woodpecker, which was caused by a nationwide loss of habitat, the drop in waterfowl populations here is a local problem, caused not by a loss of habitat but by the opposite—an increase in habitat. As northern wildlife refuges (and farmers) beefed up their winter crops, more food became available to migrating waterfowl. And unlike the snowbirds that flock down I-95 in winter, a lack of food, not cold weather, drives waterfowl south. So the birds began "short-stopping," wintering on chilly Yankee refuges well north of their usual stopping places. The practice helps them conserve energy and makes sense—if not to snowbirds, then at least to waterfowl.

Beyond Pool D, the trail crosses Visitors Drive and parallels the eastern shore of Martins Lake. A few ducks quack on the other side of the lake, but they are too far away to see. The path becomes a low boardwalk, which leads into a bog filled with bays and loblolly pines and towering Atlantic white cedars. The thin, reddish bark of the cedars appears twisted and spirals up from the ground to small, dark-green crowns. Near an observation platform at the end of the trail, we find seats on a mushroom encrusted log. While we rest, I examine the mushrooms, some of which resemble seashells.

Winter is not usually mushroom season, but these are bracket or shelf mushrooms, tough, leathery fungi that can tolerate mild winters. These are clam-shaped and white, about an inch-and-a-half wide, with concentric lines that mimic the growth ridges of a clam shell. Using a field guide, I determine that they are members of the polypore family, and based on an illustration in the guide, probably *Polyporus conchifer*. But field identification of mushrooms is tricky. Inedible varieties in particular, such as most bracket mushrooms, get short shrift, so I wouldn't bet the farm on *P. conchifer*. But the ambiguity doesn't bother me; regardless of their species, I know what the pale little rascals on the log are doing, and it is work essential to the life of the forest.

In their immobility, fungi resemble plants, and at one time, they were considered members of the plant kingdom. However, they differ from plants in one very important way: fungi lack chlorophyll; they cannot photosynthesize energy from sunlight.

Like animals, they must eat to survive. But fungi share few other characteristics with the members of the animal kingdom, so biologists have assigned them their own domain: Kingdom Fungi.

Mushrooms are members of Kingdom Fungi, and they come in three basic models (although gourmands would argue that there are only two—edible and inedible). Saprophytic mushrooms live on dead organic matter, much as we humans do; parasitic mushrooms attack living organisms; and mycorrhizal mushrooms are symbiotes. It takes only a short walk in the woods to tell where mushrooms such as *P. conchifer* fit; they are always attached to dead (or nearly dead) trees, so they are clearly saprophytes.

Saprophytic mushrooms are important to the forest because they hasten the decomposition of dead vegetation and make the dirt from which new life springs. But many of them are also critical to the survival of individual species. One specialized saprophyte, for example, lives off the dead heartwood in living trees. That fungus, *Phellinus pini*, causes red heart, the disease that makes the red-cockaded woodpecker's laborious nest excavations easier.

After our rest, we start back toward Lake Bee. The sky darkens further, and it begins to rain. We plod along, heads down. A stray dog, an all-white spitz, joins us. The dog frolics around us, licking our fingers and raising our spirits. Diane immediately names him "Spot."

About halfway back, Spot suddenly takes off toward Pool D. He pauses beneath a large oak on the shore of the lake. The lake, the bare tree, and the sky are ominously gray, but in the tree above the white dog is a patch of shocking green. It is a striking tableau, a pen-and-ink sketch with one bright splotch of paint. The dog paws at the ground around the base of the tree for a moment, then heads back toward us, leaving me staring at the ball of green. It is, of course, mistletoe, also known as the "Christmas plant," and it has had a powerful effect on humans for centuries.

Because it is evergreen and fruits in the winter, mistletoe has been a symbol of fertility since the time of the Druids. The custom of kissing under a sprig of mistletoe, is likely a toned-down version of what the Druids did beneath its branches in lustier times. According to Pliny, the Gauls used mistletoe as a cure for sterility. The English believed it could relieve epilepsy, St. Vitus's dance, and other diseases. The remedial power of mistletoe was tested in 1864 by a Dr. Bull, who concluded that extracts of the plant had only a "slight tonic" effect. One aspect of mistletoe extract did impress him, though. He described its taste as "nauseous" and "bitterish." Not satisfied that he had gotten his message across, Dr. Bull went on to coin one of the great words in the literature of flavors, further describing the extract as "sub-austere."

Although much of the folklore about mistletoe comes from Europe, over one thousand species of these plants are scattered over the earth. It thrives from snowy Asia to equatorial Africa. Unlike saprophytic fungi, virtually all mistletoes are parasites, taking what they need from a host tree and sometimes killing it.

The mistletoe found in the South, *Phorandendron serotinium*, however, is a more polite, less destructive species that generates its own food through photosynthesis and takes only water from its host. *P. serotinium* roots on the branches of flowering trees. It doesn't appear to harm the trees on which it grows, except in periods of drought, when the water taken by the mistletoe further stresses them. It is present year-round, but it is more easily spotted in winter when its evergreen leaves contrast boldly with the stark gray of its deciduous hosts.

By the time we get back to the car, the rain has stopped, and the day lightens up a bit. As we sit on a picnic table feeding Spot peanut-butter-and-cheese crackers, a *tap-tap-tap* comes from a tree near the shore of Lake Bee. A ladder-backed woodpecker with white cheek pouches is working a longleaf pine less than fifty feet from us. It is a red-cockaded woodpecker, and it pecks away at the trunk of the tree for a minute or more before flying away. This kind of thing often happens to naturalists; after hours in the woods, you find what you've been looking for in a picnic area.

I slide off the bench and walk to the pine. It's base is charred by fire. In this forest, a fire-blackened trunk is a more appropriate symbol of fertility than mistletoe. It is a sign of the rebirth of the longleaf-pine forest—and, consequently, the red-cockaded woodpecker. Setting fires to destroy hardwoods appears to be an odd way to re-create a primeval forest. But the lesson to be learned here is an old one, the same one taught by the fungus that causes red heart: in nature, life originates with death as inevitably as death originates with life.

BEFORE YOU GO

For More Information

Carolina Sandhills National Wildlife Refuge
Route 2, Box 330
McBee, S.C. 29101
(803) 335-8401

Accommodations

The closest accommodations are in Hartsville. Contact

Greater Hartsville Chamber of Commerce
P.O. Box 578
Hartsville, S.C. 29551
(803) 332-6401

Campgrounds

Camping is not permitted in the refuge. The closest public campground is at Sand Hills State Forest, which is adjacent to the refuge. For information, contact

Sand Hills State Forest
Box 128
Patrick, S.C. 29584
(803) 498-6478

Maps

Tate's Trail is well marked, and the map in the free refuge brochure is all that's needed for this walk.

Additional Reading

The Biology of Mistletoes edited by Malcolm Calder and Peter Bernhardt, Academic Press, New York, 1983.

"Born of Fire, Under Fire" by Jerome A. Jackson, *Birder's World* 7, December 1993, 12-16.

Mushrooms of North America by Orson K. Miller, Jr., E. P. Dutton & Co., Inc., New York.

"Restoring a 'Grass-Roots' Ecosystem" by Carolee Boyles-Sprenkel, *American Forests* 99, May/June 1993, 43-45.

A Stillness in the Pines: The Ecology of the Red-Cockaded Woodpecker by Robert W. McFarlane, W.W. Norton & Company, New York, 1992.

The Winter's Tale by William Shakespeare from *The Complete Works of William Shakespeare*, Garden City Books, Garden City, New York, 1936.

THE PIEDMONT

Beavers inhabit all the northern continent of America, . . . they are the most sagacious and provident of all other quadrupeds; their economy and inimitable art in building their houses would puzzle the most skillful architect . . .

Mark Catesby, 1731

CHEROKEE TERRITORY

Raven Rock Hiking Trail
Keowee-Toxaway State Park

Keowee-Toxaway State Park is 15 miles northwest of Pickens, just off S.C. 11. The 1,000-acre park has two entrances, one north of the highway, the other south of it. Raven Rock Hiking Trail starts in a parking lot behind the Meeting House near the north entrance. The trail (the first and last leg of which are called the Natural Bridge Nature Trail in the park map) is described here as a counterclockwise loop. It starts east through a typical Piedmont forest, then curls north toward Lake Keowee. At 2.2 miles, the path crosses a burned area. The blue-blazed trail turns right and descends to the shore of the lake, but another trail, unmarked but easy to follow, plows straight ahead for 0.1 mile to Raven Rock, a rocky bluff overlooking the lake. From Raven Rock, return to the main trail, which south to Poe Creek, crosses it, and climbs back to a parking lot in front of the Meeting House.

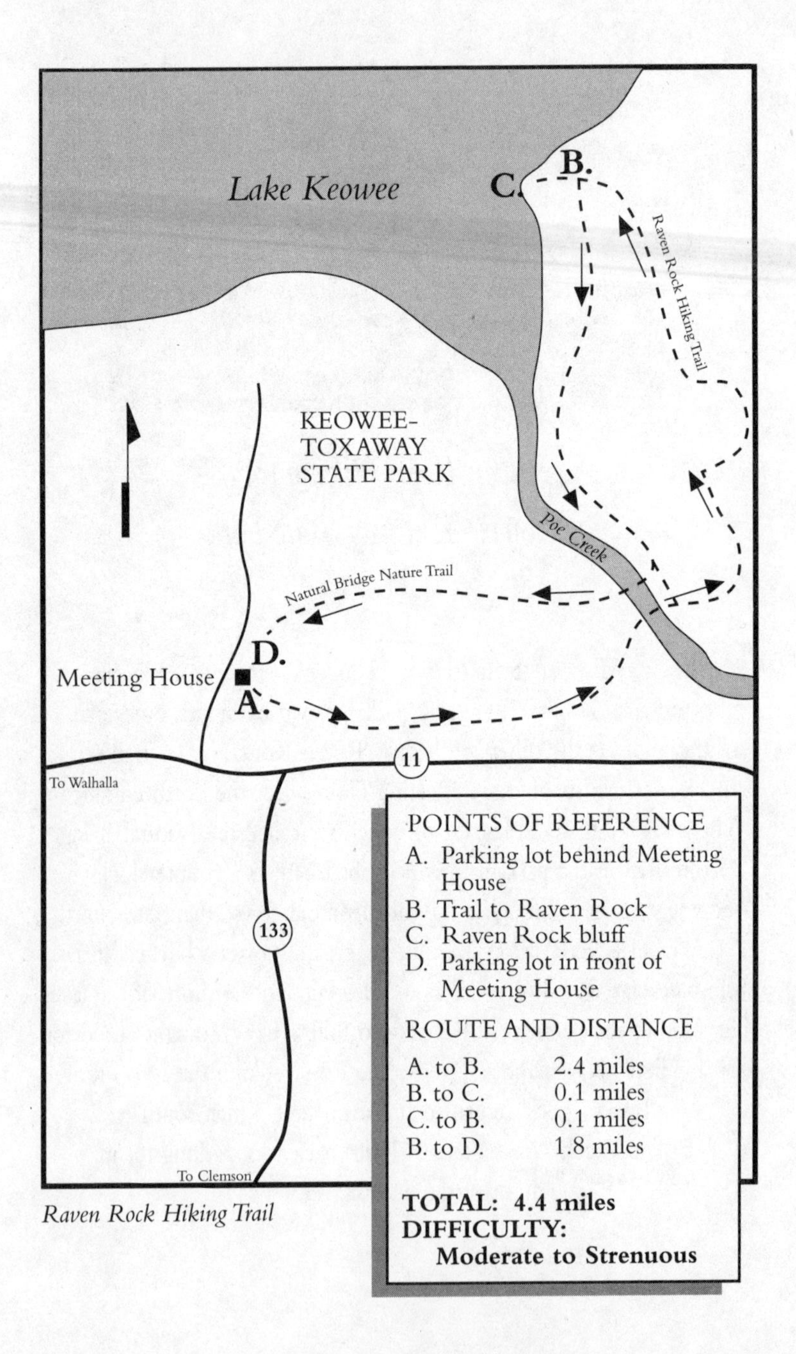

Raven Rock Hiking Trail

Cherokee Territory

Keowee-Toxaway Park is one of the state's best-kept secrets, ranking well below its neighbors—Table Rock, Oconee, and Caesars Head—in number of visitors. Its modest popularity may stem from its enigmatic nature, for this is a difficult park to classify, one that calls for a subtle eye and a willingness to look at things twice. The park's history is equally elusive; its tales of soldiers and Indians lie below the surface, waiting to be pried loose.

One reason for the park's confusing character is its location. Keowee-Toxaway sits squarely on the line that divides the state's mountain province from the Piedmont. Ask Mack Copeland, the park superintendent, who is intimately familiar with this land, into which province he would place it, and he will not answer you directly but say only that "We're not exactly in the mountains, we're in the foothills of the mountains." You will follow that with "Ah, you're in the Piedmont, then?" and Mack will answer, "Not necessarily." It is, in fact, a place that's hard to get a handle on, but the way to start is by walking the park's longest footpath, the 4.4-mile Raven Rock Hiking Trail.

I begin the trail on a bright and clear July morning. It has been a dry, hot summer, and the drought has caused the leaves of some of the tulip poplars near trailhead to yellow and fall. The path starts downhill through a young, but typical, Piedmont oak-hickory forest. Red oaks, white oaks, and post oaks join hickories and an occasional pine in the canopy. Dogwoods, red maples, and a smattering of mountain laurels make up the understory.

The trail continues to descend until it reaches Poe Creek. Beside the rushing waters, the oaks and hickories give way to hemlock and rhododendron and sassafras, with wild iris growing near the trail. This type of vegetation is usually found in the low-altitude forests of the southern Appalachians. In less than a mile, Keowee-Toxaway has whipsawed me, has taken me from the Piedmont to the mountains. I decide to withhold judgment on the mountains versus Piedmont question until I have finished the trail.

Beyond the creek, the path steepens, with sharp uphill and downhill pitches. Sweat begins to flow, and my shirt sticks damply to my back. On paper, this is a pussycat of a trail, but walking it is a different story. I begin to get a glimmering of why Allen de Hart rated it as strenuous in *South Carolina Hiking Trails*.

The path soon crosses a small granite outcropping littered with huge lichen-spattered boulders. The soil near the outcropping is raw red Piedmont clay, covered by an inch or so of detritus. In this clayey ground grow table mountain pines and blackjack oaks, gnarled and stunted, isolated from one another and blown into odd shapes by the wind.

Table mountain pines (*Pinus pungens*) occur only in the Appalachian region. Old-timers called it the poverty pine, a name that speaks volumes about its normal habitat. Blackjack oaks (*Quercus marilandica*), on the other hand, are found throughout the state except in the high mountains. They are small, ragged trees, rarely exceeding thirty feet in height, and their presence is said to indicate poor soil. Blackjack oaks are sometimes called scrub oaks, and like poverty pine, the name tells you a lot about the tree and the land where it grows. Forests containing both species are not common, and their presence tells me that this site is either in the upper Piedmont or in the lower ranges of the mountain province—but not which one.

Beyond the granite outcropping, the trail gets rougher, with even more precipitous ups and downs. The sweet warmth of early morning has turned into a midmorning furnace. Sweat fogs my glasses and drips from my nose. Through the fog, I glimpse a conoidal mass, an oversized toy top hanging at eye level from the branch of a sweet gum beside the trail. It is gray and papery, over a foot long, and heavy enough to bend the branch of the tree to which it is attached.

Black insects with yellowish faces and white-spotted abdomens buzz around it, land near an opening at its base, and parade through a passageway into the nest. I lean closer to get a better look. The buzzing grows louder and higher pitched. I back away; fortunately, it doesn't take a close examination to figure out what these insects are. In this part of the country, only bald-faced hornets (*Vespula maculata*) build nests like this one.

Though bald-faced hornets are not particularly aggressive, all colonial-nesting insects can get a bit, well, waspish when their nests are threatened. And since I have no desire to race a swarm of angry hornets, I move on quickly.

A half-mile later, the trail passes a burned area. Blue blazes lead to the right, marking the trail down to the shores of Lake Keowee, but I follow an equally well-used path to a rocky bluff overlooking the lake. I plop down on a twenty-foot expanse of granite known as Raven Rock and look out over the cool, green waters.

Keowee-Toxaway State Park is named for the Keowee River and its tributary the Toxaway River. The Keowee used to flow through a valley now covered by the lake in front of me. Duke Power Company dammed the Keowee in 1968 to generate hydroelectric power and provide cooling water for its Oconee Nuclear Station.

Scenic South Carolina, a book written by Eugene Sloan and published two years before the dam was built, contains several black-and-white photographs of the area and describes the Keowee as a "beautiful river valley," where "the scenery has been little spoiled by mankind." Perhaps to atone for deep-sixing such scenery, Duke Power donated the land for Keowee-Toxaway State Park in 1970.

A high-pitched whine interrupts my contemplation of the lake. From the corner of my eye, I see the blur of a big fast-moving bug. It's flying so fast that I can't even guess what it is. Then, suddenly, it appears two feet in front of my face, an absolutely motionless body suspended in midair on wings that beat so rapidly they are invisible.

At first glance, this yellow-and-black apparition resembles the hornets I saw earlier, or perhaps even a honeybee. But, as so often happens in this park, a longer look tells a different story. This creature has too much yellow on its abdomen to be a hornet, and it's far too chunky to be a bee. And neither bees nor hornets can hover, dead-still in the air, as this bug is doing. My mind fumbles for an identification, and the word "hover" finally triggers a synaptic response. Hover fly, I think to myself. This is a hover fly.

Of course, hover flies move faster than my brain, and by the time its name surfaces, the fly has disappeared. Though I still hear its whine, I have no idea where it is. This check-you-out-and-vanish behavior is typical of hover flies, which exhibit, according to author Sue Hubbell, a kind of "buggish curiosity" about people.

Hover flies are members of the family Syrphidae and the order Diptera, also called the order of true flies. Flies differ from other insects in that they have only one pair of wings. In the case of syrphid flies, that's enough; even with only one pair, they are fast-moving aerial acrobats. The fly that inspected me on Raven Rock, an American hover fly (*Metasyrphus americanus*), is a good example of the breed; it zipped about so quickly that it seemed to dematerialize in one spot and materialize, almost instantly, in another.

House flies—because they feed on manure and rotting food and transmit diseases—have given all flies a bad name. In the case of the American hover fly, however, the rap is undeserved. In fact, *M. americanus* doesn't resemble a house fly at all; it is more like a bee in both appearance and eating habits.

It is a generally black, bee-sized bug, with a yellowish head and three yellow bands around its abdomen. Like bees and hornets, it drinks nectar from flowers, but unlike them, it has no stinger. It is a valuable insect; the adults pollinate flowers and the larvae eat the aphids that attack crops and other plants.

American hover flies are also friendly and will (supposedly) light on your finger, if you extend one toward them. Unfortunately, by the time I recall this snippet of lore, even the whine of the fly's wings has become inaudible, and I am alone on my rock in the midday sun. When I get up to start the walk back, I notice that the spot where I have been sitting is damp with sweat.

After a short uphill climb, the trail begins a long descent back to Poe Creek. At the creek, the trail turns southeast and parallels the stream for a while. The path here is overhung with rhododendron, and it's moist and dark and thankfully cool. The creek is clear and fast-flowing, with a few small white-water cascades. I cross to the east bank to begin the final leg of the walk, a steep uphill back to trailhead. The creek, hills, and rhododendron again remind me of the southern Appalachians, and of the Indians that once occupied that territory. To me, terrain like this suggests Cherokee country—which, of course, this once was.

When the rising waters of Lake Keowee flooded this valley, they covered more than just a patch of pretty scenery. Down there, at the bottom of this eighteen-thousand-acre lake, is the site of Keowe, once a prominent Cherokee village.

The decline of the Cherokee is a sad, familiar story, but one little-known aspect of it was the role played by the village of Keowe. Keowe was once the largest Cherokee village in South

Carolina, the capital of the Lower Cherokee Nation. The village's problems started in 1753 when the English and French began warming up for the French and Indian War.

James Glen, governor of the South Carolina colony, proposed building a fort in Cherokee territory, ostensibly to protect the Cherokees from their enemies the Creeks. His real purpose, however, was to keep the Lower Cherokees in the English orbit, out of the hands of the French and the more independent Middle Cherokees, a group centered in Tennessee. He got the Lower Cherokees' permission to proceed, and by December 1753, the Union Jack was flying over Fort Prince George, a tiny stockade located at a ford on the east bank of the Keowee River. On the other side of the river was the Cherokee village of Keowe.

Within two years, the Middle Cherokees and the Virginia colonists were fighting a vicious undeclared war. The reasons for the fighting have been lost in the haze of history, but there were ambushes, massacres, and horse thievery on both sides. Relations between the South Carolinians and the Lower Cherokees, however, remained reasonably good until 1759. In the early fall of that year, three officers from Fort Prince George, which was by then considerably larger than its original size, crossed the Keowee River and brutally assaulted three Indian women. The Lower Cherokees retaliated, and William Henry Lyttleton, the new governor of South Carolina, responded by calling up fourteen hundred militiamen.

Among the Cherokees, calmer heads finally prevailed. A delegation of thirty-one Indians, led by the young war chief Oconostota, rode to Charles Town—a trip of almost 250 miles—to defuse the crises. Governor Lyttleton declined to meet with them and later seized the group, transferring them to Fort Prince George and imprisoning them in a room designed to sleep six soldiers. Lyttleton, who had accompanied the prisoners to the fort, then released Oconostota and a few others, and returned to Charles Town, congratulating himself on a job well done. Oconostota immediately laid siege to Fort Prince George.

After a few weeks, Oconostota sent word that he wanted to talk. Lieutenant Coytmore, the commander of the fort agreed. As soon as the lieutenant stepped outside the stockade, he was shot by Oconostota's warriors, who had concealed themselves near the entrance. The soldiers inside promptly retaliated, murdering all twenty-four of the remaining Indian prisoners. It was now, as Indian ethnologist James Mooney put it, "war to the end."

Because of the whites' overwhelming numerical superiority, it was a war the Cherokees could not win. In September 1761, they surrendered. In just a few years, the Cherokees had lost almost all of their villages and over one-half of their warriors. There is no record of what happened to the village of Keowe during the war, but it was almost certainly deserted by the time it was over. The next mention of Keowe and its neighboring fort comes from William Bartram, the peripatetic Philadelphia naturalist, who visited the area fifteen years later:

> This fertile vale [of Keowee] within the remembrance of some old traders with whom I conversed, was one continued settlement; the swelling sides of the adjoining hills were then covered with habitations, and the rich level grounds lying on the river, was cultivated and planted, which now exhibit a very different spectacle, humiliating indeed to the present generation, the posterity and feeble remains of the once potent and renowned Cherokees: the vestiges of the ancient Indian dwellings are yet visible on the feet of the hills bordering and fronting on the vale. . . .

> There are several Indian mounts or tumuli, and terraces, monuments of the ancients, at the site of Keowe, near the fort Prince George, but no Indian habitations at present; and here are several dwellings inhabited by white people concerned in the Indian trade . . .

The Cherokees' misfortunes did not end with the destruction of Keowe. In 1838, ten years after gold was discovered on Cherokee land in northern Georgia, many of them were brutally marched to Oklahoma, over a route known as the Trail of Tears. But a few escaped the "removal" to form the nucleus of an eastern band. Today, many of their descendants live on the Qualla Reservation near Great Smoky Mountains National Park, where they farm, run businesses, and cheerfully hawk Taiwanese-made "Genuine Indian Moccasins" to palefaces headed into the park. They also operate the Museum of the Cherokee Indian, which offers a serious look at the history and culture of this powerful and resilient tribe.

By the time I reach the end of the trail, the heat is suffocating. I strip off my shirt. There's not a dry thread in it. I grab a towel, sit on a shady picnic table, dry off, then drape the damp towel over my head. Well, what about the question I started the day with? Is Keowee-Toxaway in the mountains or the Piedmont? I know that Piedmont is Italian for "the foot of the hills," so I base my decision, not on what I've seen, not on the presence or absence of red clay or table mountain pines or blackjack oaks, and not even on what I've learned from Mack Copeland. I return to the man

who was almost certainly a better naturalist than either of us. I pull out Bartram's *Travels*, to double check the quote, and there it is: "the vestiges of the ancient Indian dwellings are yet visible on the feet of the hills." I peer out from beneath the towel and look at the land. This, by god, is the Piedmont!

BEFORE YOU GO

For More Information

Keowee-Toxaway State Park
108 Residence Drive
Sunset, S.C. 29685
(803) 868-2605

Accommodations

The park has one rental unit, a three-bedroom cabin on the shores of Lake Keowee. Call the park office for reservations.

Aside from the park's cabin, the nearest lodging is in Pickens, but the choices are limited to a few bed-and-breakfasts and rental cottages. Easley, seven miles southeast of Pickens, has two motels. For information, contact

Pickens Chamber of Commerce
P.O. Box 153
Pickens, S.C. 29671
(803) 878-3258

Campgrounds

Keowee-Toxaway has twenty-four campsites situated on a hill in a fine oak-hickory forest. For information, contact the park.

Maps

The blue-blazed Raven Rock Hiking Trail is well marked, and the trail map in the free park brochure is adequate for this walk.

Points of Interest

The ¼-mile Cherokee Interpretive Trail lies near the park superintendent's office, south of S.C. 11. The trail connects the park's small museum with four outdoor exhibits that, taken together, give an overview of the life and history of the Lower Cherokee, the Indian tribe that once lived in the Keowee River valley.

Additional Reading

Broadsides from the Other Orders: A Book of Bugs by Sue Hubbell, Random House, New York, 1993.

Historical Sketch of the Cherokee by James Mooney, Aldine Publishing Company, Chicago, 1975. This book was excerpted from the "Myths of the Cherokees," an essay written by Mooney and first published in the Nineteenth Annual Report (1897-1898) of the Bureau of American Ethnology.

As an ethnologist, James Mooney worked with a number of Indian tribes, but the Cherokees interested him the most. He spent a great deal of time in their villages, learning their language and familiarizing himself with their culture, and wrote numerous monographs and essays about them.

Scenic South Carolina by Eugene B. Sloan, The State Printing Company, Columbia, 1966.

South Carolina: A Synoptic History for Laymen by Lewis P. Jones, Sandlapper Publishing, Inc., Orangeburg, South Carolina, 1971.

South Carolina: The Making of a Landscape by Charles F. Kovacik and John J. Winberry, University of South Carolina Press, Columbia, 1989. This useful book on the geography of South Carolina was first published in 1988 by Westview Press, Inc. of Boulder, Colorado.

Travels of William Bartram by William Bartram, edited by Mark Van Doren, Dover Publications, New York, 1955. This book was originally published in Philadelphia in 1791 under the title, *Travels Through North & South Carolina, Georgia, East & West Florida, The Cherokee Country, The Extensive Territories of the Muscogulges, Or Creek Confederacy, And The Country Of The Chactaws.*

ALONG THE FALL LINE

Lick Fork Lake and Horn Creek Trails
Edgefield Ranger District, Sumter National Forest

Lick Fork Lake Recreation Area lies near the eastern border of the 64,000-acre Edgefield Ranger District in Sumter National Forest. It is 12 miles west of the town of Edgefield and just south of S.C. 23. The walk starts from the north end of the recreation area's parking lot, on the Lick Fork Lake Trail. The trail first curls west around the northern end of Lick Fork Lake, then turns south and runs along the western edge of the lake. Just below the dam, Lick Fork Lake Trail intersects with Horn Creek Trail. Take Horn Creek Trail south, then east through a mixed forest of pines and hardwoods. At a gravel road (Forest Service Road 634), the path turns north and then west to a second intersection with Lick Fork Lake Trail, which runs north along the east side of the lake back to the parking area.

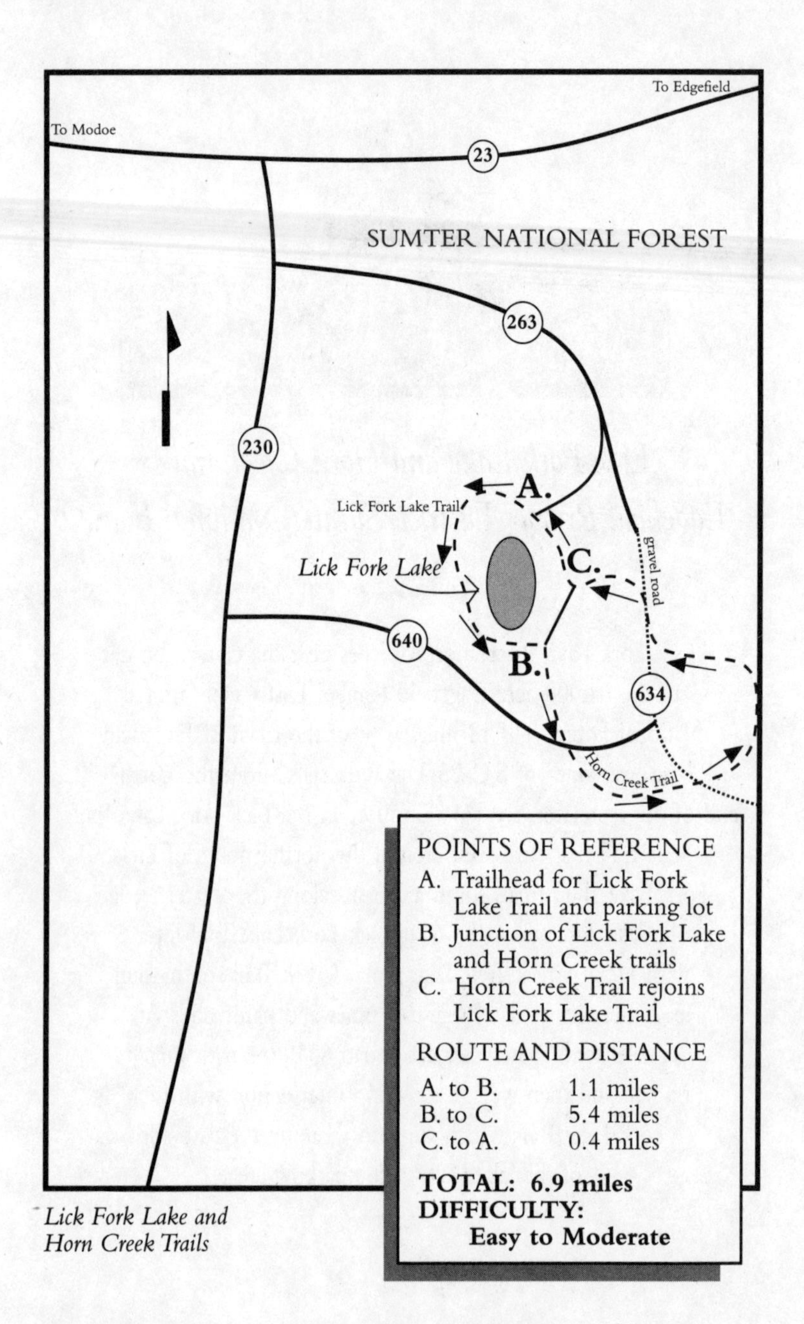

Lick Fork Lake and Horn Creek Trails

Along the Fall Line

The earliest European settlements in eastern North America were along the Atlantic coast. But, driven by a desire to colonize new land and expand trade with the Indians, settlers soon pushed inland, usually by sailing up the rivers. Their westerly penetration was stopped by the first rapids or waterfalls they encountered. Today, if one connects the stopping points of those early settlers on a map, the result is an irregular line that starts in New York City and winds its way south and then west to Montgomery, Alabama. This line is known as the fall line, and it marks the boundary between the rolling hills of the Piedmont and the flatlands of the coastal plain of the eastern United States.

The stopping points soon became outposts, then grew into commercial centers, and finally developed into cities. Many of the Southeast's state capitals lie along the fall line, including Columbia, Raleigh, and Richmond. Except for a few coastal areas, the land along the line is some of the longest-settled country in the South—and some of the most abused. The aftermath of that abuse—and the beginning of the healing process, which started early in this century—can be seen clearly on this walk through the Edgefield Ranger District of Sumter National Forest, for most of this land is within hailing distance of the fall line.

I start the Lick Fork Lake Trail on a warm, clear day in late September, when some of the trees are already beginning to show the colors of autumn. Although the trail lies near the fall line, the low, easy hills through which it winds tell you that this walk is in the Piedmont, rather than the pancake-flat coastal plain. The trees beside the narrow, well-marked path are not exclusive to the Piedmont, but they are typical of it: white oaks, beeches, and northern red oaks; dogwoods and red maples; and, of course, the pines—the towering loblollies and short-leaf pines that loom over the hardwoods. It was the tenacity of those pines that began to restore these hills after years of mistreatment.

Poor farming practices (among other things) caused the Great Depression to start in the South nearly a decade before it hit the rest of the country. The roots of these practices went back to a belief, held by the earliest settlers, that the region's land and forests were an infinite resource that could be exploited forever. The first wave of farmers cleared land and planted crops until the soil was no longer productive, then moved on, clearing new land and repeating the cycle. Later, when virgin land was no longer available, permanent farms were established, often using slaves to tend the fields. When the Civil War ended that cruel practice, Southerners adopted the tenant system of farming. This system required a cash crop (to pay the landowner), and in this part of the country, the most profitable cash crop was cotton. Cotton so impoverished the soil that by the 1920s South Carolina farmers were forced to use more fertilizer on their crops than the farmers of any other state. In an article for *South Carolina Wildlife*, Glenn Oeland quotes a government publication from that period that characterized eight million acres, almost half of the land in the state, as "destroyed."

Poor farming practices were not the only villains; cut-and-run logging did almost as much damage. Until 1880, the mom-and-pop logging operations that were typical in the South had done little damage to the region's great timber resource. The event that opened the South for rape by the timber barons was the repeal in 1876 of the Southern Homestead Law, which had restricted purchases of federal land in the South to eighty acres per person. Since most Southerners—including the lumbermen—were broke after the Civil War they could not afford to buy the land that was now available to them. Instead, Northerners gobbled up huge tracts of virgin timber at the standard price of $1.25 per acre. Flotillas of logs were soon pouring down Southern rivers to huge carpetbagger sawmills. By 1924, 90 percent of the great Southern forests were gone—and so were the lumbermen.

But the seeds of redemption were blowing in the wind. With the land farmed out and the loggers gone, native loblolly and short-leaf pines began reclaiming the denuded slopes, stemming erosion, and smoothing the old cotton furrows. The tall pines along this trail testify to the efficacy of the process; they were naturally seeded when a farm that produced cotton here was abandoned in 1905. If ever a tree deserved its nickname, it is the loblolly, known to old-timers as the "old-field pine."

Beyond the pines, the trail turns north, crosses a creek that feeds Lick Fork Lake, then curls south along the western edge of the lake. The path is narrow and soft, cushioned with pine needles. Beneath the canopy grow dark-green hollies and Christmas ferns, set off nicely by bright clumps of purple beauty berries.

The path then climbs forty feet or so above the lake, and the ground slopes steeply down to the water. Although the land is healing itself, erosion, once started, is like a cancer and is almost as hard to cure. So it is no surprise to see that runoffs from heavy rains have etched gullies two- and three-feet deep in the red clay. Many of these have been partially dammed with sandbags, the work of the Youth Conservation Corps and other organizations in 1981. Other dam builders have also been at work here, but the beavers left no sandbags, only gnawed stumps that look like sharpened pencil stubs. I look for a dam or a lodge but can't find either.

Just beyond the man-made dam that created the lake, Lick Fork Lake Trail intersects with Horn Creek Trail, and I head south on it, walking beside the creek. The stream bed is rocky, the water low and clear. The forest is mostly hardwoods: maples and tulip poplars, sweet gums and ironwoods. In fact, there is more ironwood along this creek than I have ever seen in one spot. I stop to run my hand over a smooth muscular trunk.

Ironwood (*Carpinus caroliniana*) is also known as American hornbeam or water beech. Because of its name, it is sometimes confused with American hophornbeam (*Ostrya virginiana*), which is also called ironwood. But the confusion exists only on paper; in the field, there can be no mistaking the two species. American hornbeam has a smooth blue-gray trunk, while the hophornbeam's trunk is brown and rough.

Ironwood is a short, shrubby tree. Because of its size, it has no value as lumber, and even the most rabid timber baron wouldn't give it a second glance. Its wood is very tough and very heavy, though, and it was used extensively by early settlers to make levers and handles, small items where hardness and durability were important. I like this little weed of a tree because of how well its name fits. It is almost impossible to rub a hard, sinewy trunk and not think "ironwood!"

The trail leads away from the creek and the ironwood grove, climbs to the top of a low ridge, and winds down the other side. Up here, away from the rich bottomland, the trees are smaller and scraggly. I hear chickadees and woodpeckers in the distance. A gray squirrel scoots down the middle of the path, and an orange-brown butterfly flits erratically among the weeds.

A sizable maple stands beside the trail, its trunk riddled with parallel rows of small holes about one-quarter-inch deep. The holes are so precisely spaced, the rows so perfectly horizontal that one suspects they were drilled as part of a scientific experiment. But I know better; a Norway spruce outside my house has holes in it just like these, and I know who the culprit is. Only the yellow-bellied sapsucker creates a pattern like this.

The yellow-bellied sapsucker (*Sphyrapicus varius*) is about the size of a red-cockaded woodpecker. Both sexes have white wing stripes and red patches on their heads, but only males sport the unmistakable red throat patches. These birds are winter visitors to South Carolina, migrating down from the north in the fall. I've seen only a few of them in my life, not because they are uncommon, but because they are so hard to spot. Compared to other woodpeckers, sapsuckers are quiet, wary birds, described in field guides as "unobtrusive" or "furtive." I've barely glimpsed the one that works the spruce near my house. As soon as he spots me, he scoots around to the far side of the tree and vanishes.

Sapsuckers suck or lick sap from the small holes they drill in the living cambium layer of trees. In the South, they seem to prefer sweet gums and maples (at least those are the trees where I most often find their holes), but in a pinch almost any tree will do. Sapsuckers return again and again to the same tree, and they are the only woodpeckers that can actually kill one, occasionally girdling a trunk with their neat, shallow holes. Sapsucker holes also serve as entry points for diseases, but dendrologists believe that trees rarely die from these wounds, a conclusion that my riddled, but healthy, spruce would support.

Beyond the perforated maple, the trail levels out and runs beside another creek. The creek turns into a broad slough, then back into a creek again. I look for the beaver dam that must have created the slough, but the brush is so thick along the edge of the creek, I can't see it. In this watery realm, sycamores and swamp chestnut oaks, river birches, and water oaks replace the pines and hardwoods of the upland. I cross several more creeks and finally enter a mixed pine and hardwood forest similar to the one near trailhead. To my right, beyond the forest, a patch of hillside has been clear-cut and burned. The black scar reminds me that this is not a National Park but a National *Forest*.

These days, almost no one is satisfied with the Forest Service. Many of the cries of outrage come from conservationists in the West because of the way the Forest Service carries out its mission—as assigned by the United States Congress—to manage the national forests for "multiple uses." Multiple-use management means that mining, cattle grazing, and logging—so called "extractive" practices—are permitted on some lands. This puts the Forest Service in conflict with conservationists, who would like to see them place more emphasis on recreational use of the land and on better maintaining the integrity of the ecosystems entrusted to them. In the West, this war is marked by suspicion, name calling, and lawsuits. Although Southern conservationists have the same goals as Westerners, we have a much more cordial relationship with the Forest Service.

One reason for this is that Southern national forests don't have the same pressures on them that western forests do. Southern forests are not suitable for cattle grazing and usually have no minerals worth mining. There is also less timber and, therefore, less logging. But the roots of the dichotomy go back to the way the national forests were created.

Nineteen years after establishing Yellowstone, the country's first national park, congress passed the Forest Reserve Act of 1891. It authorized the president to set aside portions of the public domain as forest reserves. President Benjamin Harrison protected the first land under this act, and by the time he left office in 1893, forest reserves totaled thirteen million acres.

But it wasn't until 1901, following the assassination of President William McKinley, that the national forest system found the friend it needed. In that year, Vice-president Teddy Roosevelt became president. In the next seven years, Roosevelt—working closely with Gifford Pinchot, chief of the Division of Forestry and founder of the modern forest service—set aside 138 million acres of land for national parks and forests, all carved out of the public domain. Since there was little land left in the public domain in the East, virtually all of these parks and forests were located in the western states.

It wasn't until 1911, when congress passed the Weeks Law, that the Forest Service was allowed to purchase private land for national forests. The law was aimed at saving the rapidly deteriorating forests and watersheds of New England and the South. Unlike the situation in the West, where the Forest Service took over virgin forests and licensed private businesses to plunder them by logging and grazing and mining the land, in the South, they *bought* beat-up, farmed-out, logged-out land with the objective of returning it to good health. So, it's no wonder that Southern conservationists look at the Forest Service in a friendlier way than Westerners. In the West, they are seen as aiding the exploiters of the land; in the South, they are considered the saviors of it—second in importance only to old-field pines.

But even in the South, the Forest Service's reservoir of good will is running low, and clear-cuts, like the one along this trail, are one of the reasons. The Service is aware of this, and they have been wrestling with more ecologically sensitive approaches to multiple-use management. How well they succeed in keeping the public on their side will depend on what the new policies are. Recent studies at the University of Georgia indicate that some ecosystems *never* fully recover after clear-cutting, so one change that would go a long way toward keeping me in their camp would be to eliminate that practice in national forests.

Near the end of the trail, the path passes through a fine mixed forest of oaks, maples, and pines. The canopy here is so thick that the ground is almost free of understory. In the spring, wildflowers would tell me what the plants in the low-lying herbaceous layer are, but absent their blooms, I can only guess. As I look down, trying to sort out species, a three-inch-long millipede crawls from the roots of wild grapes and jessamine, crosses the path, and vanishes in the detritus of the forest floor.

Maybe the ecologists at the University of Georgia were too pessimistic. This forest appears healthy. It was clear-cut eighty or ninety years ago and wasn't protected until 1936, when Sumter

National Forest was established. So, maybe clear-cuts *do* eventually heal themselves. I think back to the virgin forests I've seen, and when I look around again, I see what is missing. There are no dead trees on the ground, no mushrooms busy decomposing them, no termites at work, no beetles laying eggs in the rotting wood. These life forms—and others, too small to see—are just as important to a healthy ecosystem as millipedes and loblolly pines.

Still, I can't help but believe that, given time, most ecosystems, even those here on the much-abused land along the fall line, will eventually re-create themselves. Maybe it will take another century, or two, for some of the big trees to succumb to the sapsuckers, topple over, and begin the slow, complicated process of becoming dirt. But it will happen. All we have to do is leave the land alone. Of course, that's a difficult policy for managers imbued in the active practice of multiple-use management to follow. But the Forest Service was smart enough to start this land on the road to recovery. All they have to do now is figure out how to leave it alone long enough for time to finish the job.

BEFORE YOU GO

For More Information

Edgefield Ranger District
Sumter National Forest
321 Bacon Street
Edgefield, S.C. 29824
(803) 637-5396

Accommodations

Closest lodging is in North Augusta, about fifteen miles south of Lick Fork Lake Recreation Area. For information, contact

North Augusta Chamber of Commerce
235 Georgia Ave.
North Augusta, S.C. 29841
(803) 279-2323

Campgrounds

There are ten individual campsites and a group camping area at Lick Fork Lake. For more information, contact the Edgefield Ranger District.

Maps

Both Lick Fork Lake and Horn Creek trails are well marked. Free maps of both trails are available at the Edgefield Ranger District office.

Fees

There is a $2.00 entrance fee at Lick Fork Lake Recreation Area.

Special Precautions

Deer hunting is a popular activity in the Edgefield Ranger District. It is best to avoid these trails during hunting season, which usually runs from early October through December, or limit your visits to Sundays, when deer hunting is prohibited.

Additional Reading

"Forestry's New Frontier" by Mike Livingston, *South Carolina Wildlife* 40, November/December 1993, 16-23.

The Forest Service by Michael Frome, Westview Press, Boulder, Colorado, Second Edition 1984.

The Greening of the South: The Recovery of Land and Forest by Thomas D. Clark, The University Press of Kentucky, Lexington, 1984.

"Heritage of Hard Times" by Glenn Oeland, *South Carolina Wildlife* 39, July/August 1992, 16-29.

A Natural History of Trees of Eastern and Central North America by Donald Culross Peattie, Houghton Mifflin Company, Boston, 1948.

"Red-capped Sap-tapper" by Jerome A. Jackson, *Birder's World* 6, December 1992, 24-27.

A Sierra Club Naturalists Guide to the Piedmont by Michael A. Godfrey, Sierra Club Books, San Francisco, 1980.

South Carolina Bird Life by Alexander Sprunt, Jr., and E. Burnham Chamberlain, University of South Carolina Press, Columbia, 1949.

Long Cane Trail
Long Cane Ranger District,
Sumter National Forest

The 118,000-acre Long Cane Ranger District of Sumter National Forest lies a few miles south of Abbeville. From S.C. 28, which runs from north to south and bisects the district, go southeast on S.C. 251 for 1.7 miles to the entrance to Parson's Mountain Lake Recreation Area. The Long Cane Trail begins at a small parking lot 20 yards beyond the entrance to the campground.

The Long Cane Trail is a 22-mile loop for horses and hikers. The trail starts behind Parson's Mountain Lake campground, crosses S.C. 251 and S.C. 33, then skirts several beaver ponds. A footbridge leads across Long Cane Creek into a beautiful hardwood cove in the Long Cane Scenic Area. A sign, 3.4 miles from trailhead, marks the national champion shagbark hickory. To complete this walk, retrace your footsteps to Parson's Mountain Lake. If you decide to walk the entire loop, plow ahead quickly; you have another 19 miles to go.

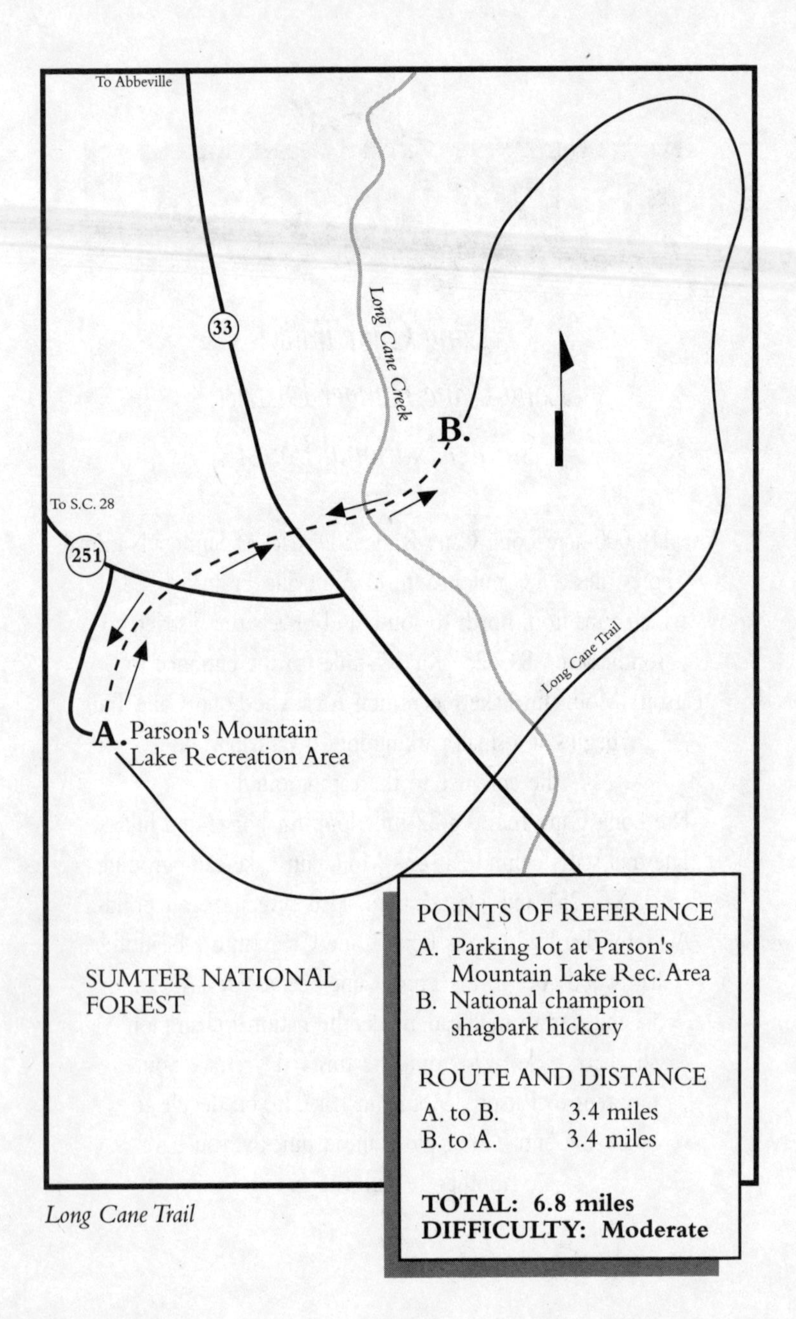

Long Cane Trail

Perfectly Piedmont

The history of the Piedmont is not pretty, at least as far as the land is concerned. Hardly a scrap of virgin forest remains. From New Jersey to Alabama, the Piedmont's rolling hills, rich soil, and moderate climate attracted European settlers like a cornfield attracts pigs. First came trading outposts, then lumber mills and farms and towns. By the 1930s, much of the Piedmont was a deforested, eroded mess.

State and federal agencies began buying up cheap, logged-over, farmed-out land to restore the forests and watersheds. In the South, much of this work fell to the Forest Service, and the results of their efforts can be seen along the Long Cane Trail in Sumter National Forest. The trail passes through land that is still being logged, although with considerably more restraint than in the past, and then enters Long Cane Scenic Area, which has been off-limits to loggers for years. There, a fine mixed-hardwood forest has reclaimed the land, and hikers can stroll through a landscape similar to the one chronicled by the great traveler and surveyor John Lawson in his 1709 book *A New Voyage to Carolina*. Lawson was one of the earliest Europeans to write about the Piedmont, and when he visited there in the early eighteenth century, the region was still so deserted that he described it as "lying betwixt the Inhabitants and the Ledges of the Mountains."

Diane and I begin the Long Cane Trail on a warm, cloudy day in mid-April. We do not intend to hike all of the trail's twenty-two miles. Our goals are more modest; we want to see the Long Cane Scenic Area and the national champion shagbark hickory that stands there, a round trip of seven miles.

The path starts on an old logging road with shin-high grass growing up between ancient ruts. Tall loblolly pines grow in the campground to the left, but the other side of the trail, which has been logged recently, is scrub—small pines, dogwoods, and poison ivy.

After crossing S.C. 251, the trail narrows and the forest changes dramatically. Here, the Forest Service's beneficial hand is evident; the land is soft-green and healthy, unmarred by erosion or recent logging. Sizable hardwoods—elms and maples and sweet gums—predominate, with only a few loblollies and red cedars scattered among them. Mockingbirds sing complicated, ever-changing songs from the trees. Butterflies float among the ferns and thistles and blueberry bushes. The country has just enough roll to let you know you are in the Piedmont.

The trail begins a slow, easy descent. A large azalea with pink trumpet-like flowers and no leaves grows beside the path. It is the well-named *Rhododendron nudiflorum*, sometimes called pinxter-flower, an uncommon deciduous wild azalea, whose leaves don't emerge until after it has bloomed.

As the trail approaches the bottomland, bigger trees begin to appear. Tulip poplars, oaks, and maples, still showing the pale-green leaves of spring, tower over an understory of blackberry bushes and ferns. Dark loblolly pines brood among the hardwoods, and thick, hairy vines of poison ivy snake up massive trunks. The path parallels a small stream. A gray squirrel scampers among smooth-barked beeches and flaky river birches that grow along its banks. We spot our first shagbark hickory, a shaggy, smoke-colored trunk topped by a dense, green crown.

Suddenly, the forest opens up, and the trail skirts a large pond of fifty or more acres bordered by bright-green rushes and cattails. Gray snags protrude from the dark water, and a goose honks in the distance. Though it looks very much at home here, the pond is a surprise.

The Pleistocene glaciers, which scraped out the northern lakes, never made it this far south, so natural lakes don't occur in the southern Piedmont. Here, a lake can mean only one thing: a dam lies downstream. Only two species build dams big enough to create a pond this size. Since there are no roads to support the cement trucks favored by one of those species, it is no surprise to find trees near the path with the bark stripped from their trunks. This is a beaver pond, the work of *Castor canadensis*, North America's largest rodent.

Beavers were once plentiful in this part of the Piedmont, and John Lawson wrote about them. "Bevers are very numerous in *Carolina*," he said, "their being an abundance of their Dams in all Parts of the Country, where I have travel'd. They are the most industrious and greatest Artificers (in building their Dams and Houses) of any four-footed Creatures in the World." By the turn of this century, though, the great Artificers had been extirpated from the South by trappers, who valued their soft, dense fur, and by farmers, who resented their habit of damming streams that flooded their bottomland farms. It was not until beavers were reintroduced in the 1920s that ponds began to reappear in the southern Piedmont.

Beaver ponds add biological diversity to Piedmont forests. In addition to the water plants that border them, beaver ponds support rich soups of microorganisms that sustain a menagerie of wildlife, from fish to frogs, from mollusks to insects.

This pond, too, must have the usual assortment of life, but the only sign of it so far is the steady *crik, crik, crik* of chorus frogs. Then, two small, compact ducks erupt from the center of the lake and fly to a nearby tree. It is not necessary to see the drake's fancy colors or the female's white eye ring to identify these birds; in South Carolina, except for the rare long-necked fulvous whistling duck, the only duck that lights in trees is the wood duck.

Linnaeus gave the wood duck its scientific name of *Aix sponsa*. *Aix* is Greek for water bird; *sponsa* is Latin for bride. One can almost see the famous Swedish naturalist puzzling over his brightly colored specimens. Clearly, these birds are waterfowl, he must have thought, but how to select an epithet to describe the species? The male's brilliant colors must have reminded him of the fancy clothes worn by brides and, mixing his genders a bit, out came *sponsa*, a fair name for one the most exquisite birds in the world. Even John Lawson, who usually confined his comments on ducks to how their flesh tasted, described the wood duck or, as he called it, the Summer Duck as "very beautiful."

Only once have I gotten close enough to a male wood duck in the wild to clearly see its brilliant plumage. It was swimming slowly in a canal ten yards from me. Its crested head was glossy black and iridescent green, with striking white markings; its wings were dark and rimmed with white; and its breast was a rich buff color. Its body appeared polished and smooth, more like a colorfully painted decoy than a live flesh-and-blood creature.

One of the snags in the pond has a hole in its trunk big enough to accommodate wood ducks, and I assume the pair I saw are nesting there. Wood ducks are born in cavities as high as fifty feet above the ground, and almost immediately after hatching, the tiny ducklings launch themselves into the air and flutter to the ground (or water) below. I scan the pond for ducklings, but if there are any, they have, like their parents, disappeared.

We follow the trail around the pond, and pass a beaver dam and another pond. The path then starts to climb away from the bottomland. Beeches, sweet gums, and red maples give way to a more typical Piedmont forest of oaks and hickories and poplars. Half a mile later, the trail descends to Long Cane Creek, a high, wide, and fast-flowing stream with soft, reddish-purple phlox growing on its banks. A narrow iron footbridge leads across the creek into the Long Cane Scenic Area.

Most of the land in the Long Cane Ranger District is logged whenever the age, size, and condition of the timber warrants it, but the scenic area has not felt the axe since the 1930s, and the land shows it. This is the real thing, a mature Piedmont forest. Huge pines and hardwoods cover the slopes. Maples and loblollies, beeches and oaks reach for sunlight, and shagbark hickories—an unusual species in much of the Piedmont—are numerous. Azaleas and trilliums and viburnums thrive in the shady, open ground beneath the trees. The country is not identical to John Lawson's Piedmont, but it's close.

By the time we reach the record shagbark hickory, the sky has darkened and the wind is up. The cooler air smells of rain. The tree is a hundred feet from the trail, and we walk downhill through soft, brown leaves and crackly twigs to stand beside it. A trailside sign modestly identifies the tree as a state record, but the 1994 edition of the National Register of Big Trees calls it a national champion, the largest shagbark hickory in the United States (and presumably the world, since the species occurs only in this country, and in the extreme fringes of southern Quebec and northern Mexico).

Champion trees fascinate me, even though I know that a record-sized tree is no more important to the ecology of a forest than any other mature specimen. Still, standing beside one of these giants never fails to affect me. The oldest living things on the planet, and the largest, are trees, and the big ones exude an aura of unperturbable strength. Standing next to one, or in a grove of them, relaxes most of us by putting the details of our short lives into larger perspective. I once watched a band of rowdy, shouting kids walk into a redwood grove; within minutes they were whispering to one another.

Though a light rain has begun to fall, I walk slowly around the old shagbark looking for nuts; I rub my hand over the rough, gray bark and look up at the dark crown. According to the register of national champions, this tree is eleven feet in circumference and over one hundred feet tall. I back away to get a better look at it. Its top is obscured by other trees, but its bark is as shaggy as its name implies, hanging from the trunk in hairy, horizontal strips with the ends of each strip curling away from the tree. Biologists named this species *Carya ovata*, but in his inventory of the trees of Carolina, John Lawson called it "the Flying-bark'd Hickory." And as I look at the tree, straight-trunked and shaggy in the soft rain, that is the name that seems appropriate.

Why is a shagbark shaggy? A partial answer can be found in the hammock experiment. Years ago, I installed a hammock in my backyard, affixing it to rings screwed into two living trees. Although the trees grew taller, the hammock never budged. The reason is that the trunk of a tree does not grow vertically (unlike the tips of its roots and branches) but expands laterally as the thin layer of cells of the cambium divide and multiply. This lateral expansion of the trunk causes the tree's dead, inelastic outer bark to slough off, usually in strips that create fissures and cracks, as in ashes, oaks, and most hickories, but occasionally in large plates of loose bark, as in the sycamore and shagbark hickory.

But the science behind this answer turns out to be only one question deep, and a follow-up to it draws a less satisfying response. Why is a shagbark hickory shaggy while a mockernut hickory isn't?

The outer bark of a tree, science mumbles, is not completely inelastic, and its residual elasticity varies from species to species, causing the bark to flake off differently. You'd get a better answer if you asked biologists to explain the cellular action in a tree's cambium layer and a poorer one if you asked it to tell you why the shagginess of shagbarks in the same forest varies so widely. (In fact, some shagbarks, called bastard hickories, are not shaggy at all.)

The difference in the quality of the answers stems from a current trend in biological research. These days, most biologists prefer to study small systems of cells rather than whole organisms.

This is called reductionism, the method of investigating large, complicated systems by studying the smaller systems which compose them. This is the opposite of what ecologists do; they observe the forest before they study a tree. But so far neither discipline can tell us why the shagbark is shaggy and the mockernut is not. This suits me fine; trees like this magnificent hickory should have some mystery about them.

By the time we begin the walk back, the rain has become a cooling mist. The shower has quieted the songbirds, and a hush lies over the forest. After a mile, the mist vanishes and the air begins to dry. An owl hoots from the deep woods, and chickadees crank up their repetitive calls in the brush. Butterflies—skippers, swallowtails, and red-spotted purples—come out from wherever they've been hiding and burrow deeply into wildflowers.

After leaving the scenic area, we pick up our pace and hurry through the less pristine parts of the forest. But the Piedmont—the home of leafless azaleas, hand-painted ducks, and shaggy hickories—has one more curiosity to show us today. Near the end of the trail, in an area exposed to the sun, stands a wildflower we missed on the walk in. It has two large umbrella-shaped leaves with a single waxy, white flower hanging from the fork between the leaves. It is a mayapple (*Podophyllum peltatum*), an oddball wildflower that produces a fruit edible by humans.

Mayapples ripen in the fall. The fruits are yellow and about the size of a small lemon. John Lawson called them Maycocks and characterized their flavor as "an agreeable Sweet, mixt with an acid taste." I tasted a mayapple once; it was so tart my mouth stayed puckered for days. I wasn't surprised, though; I've had problems before with Lawson's taste buds. I once followed his recipe for brewing yaupon tea, and the first taste was so bad that I couldn't drink a glass of Lipton's for months.

Although I don't envy John Lawson's diet (mayapples and yaupon tea were some of the more agreeable things he consumed), I am jealous of his journeys through the Piedmont. In addition to Bevers and Summer Ducks, Maycocks and Flying-bark'd Hickories—Buffelo, Panthers, and Wolves also roamed Lawson's Piedmont. These animals may never be seen again in wild here, but one can hope. The beavers are already back, and rumors about cougar sightings and wolf tracks are a dime a dozen. So far, I haven't heard any reports of buffalo returning to the Piedmont, but the next time I see an animal with horns, I'm not going to automatically think "cow."

BEFORE YOU GO

For More Information

Long Cane Ranger District
Sumter National Forest
P.O. Box 30
Edgefield, S.C. 29824
(803) 637-5396

Accommodations

Motels are available in Greenwood, about 11 miles northeast of Parson's Mountain Lake Recreation Area. Contact

Greenwood Chamber of Commerce
P.O. Box 980
Greenwood, S.C. 29648
(803) 223-8431

Campgrounds

Twenty-seven family campsites are situated under the loblolly pines at Parson's Mountain Lake Recreation Area, all available on a first-come, first-served basis.

Maps

The segment of trail covered in this walk is well marked and easy to follow. The map in the Forest Service's free brochure, "Horseback Riders' and Hikers' Guide to the Long Cane Trail," is sufficient. A more detailed map of the recreation area, "Parson's Mountain Lake Recreation Area & Trails," is useful for finding the trailhead.

Special Precautions

The Long Cane Trail is used by both hikers and horseback riders. Horses have churned up the path in a few places, so expect mud in damp weather and horse apples in any weather.

Points of Interest

Just a few hundred yards from trailhead, beside F.R. 515, stands South Carolina's largest white oak. This is a huge tree, much bigger in circumference than the pristine, world-record shagbark hickory, tucked away deep in the scenic area. Because of its location, though, vandals, who apparently prefer to operate from cars rather than on foot, have sprayed it with bright orange and red paints. The colorful trunk put me off a bit, but the tree appeared healthy and unperturbed.

Additional Reading

The Audubon Society Encyclopedia of North American Birds by John K. Terres, Wings Press, New York, 1991. This book was originally

published by Alfred A. Knopf and was last copyrighted by them in 1980.

The Growing Tree, revised edition by Brayton F. Wilson, The University of Massachusetts, Amherst, 1984.

"National Register of Big Trees," *American Forests* 100, January/February 1994, special insert 1-48.

A Natural History of Trees of Eastern and Central North America by Donald Culross Peattie, Houghton Mifflin Company, Boston, 1948.

A New Voyage to Carolina by John Lawson, edited with an introduction and notes by Hugh Talmage Lefler, The University of North Carolina Press, Chapel Hill, 1967. This book was first published in London in 1709.

The Story of Trees by Dr. Ferdinand C. Lane, Doubleday & Company, Inc., Garden City, New York, 1953.

Wildflowers in South Carolina by Wade T. Batson, University of South Carolina Press, Columbia, 1964.

Wildflowers of Eastern America by John E. Klimas and James A. Cunningham, Galahad Books, New York, 1981.

THE COASTAL PLAIN

Now at once the mountains divide; and disclose to view the ample Occonne vale, encircled by a wreath of uniform hills; their swelling bases clad in a cheerful verdure, over which, issuing from between the mountains, plays along a glittering river, . . .

William Bartram, 1791

East Fork–Chattooga River–Foothills Trail Loop
Ellicott Rock Wilderness
Andrew Pickens Ranger District, Sumter National Forest

The 79,000-acre Andrew Pickens Ranger District of Sumter National Forest lies in the northwestern corner of the state. This walk starts at the Chattooga Picnic Area, which is adjacent to the Walhalla National Fish Hatchery in northern Oconee County. From the town of Walhalla, take S.C. 107 north for 15 miles to Fish Hatchery Road and follow it until it dead ends at a parking lot. The East Fork Trail begins there.

After passing through the picnic area, the trail crosses to the north bank of East Fork, a sizable tributary of the Chattooga River. The broad, well-maintained path parallels the creek for 2.5 miles and ends at the Chattooga Trail. Follow the Chattooga Trail south for 1.0 mile, over a bridge across East Fork and then along the Chattooga River, to a fork in the trail. Go left at the fork, on the path that leads away from the river to the Foothills Trail. Take the Foothills Trail east and, after a stiff climb out of the valley, proceed along a ridgeline to Fish Hatchery Road. From there, it is 1.7 pleasant, paved, downhill miles back to the parking lot.

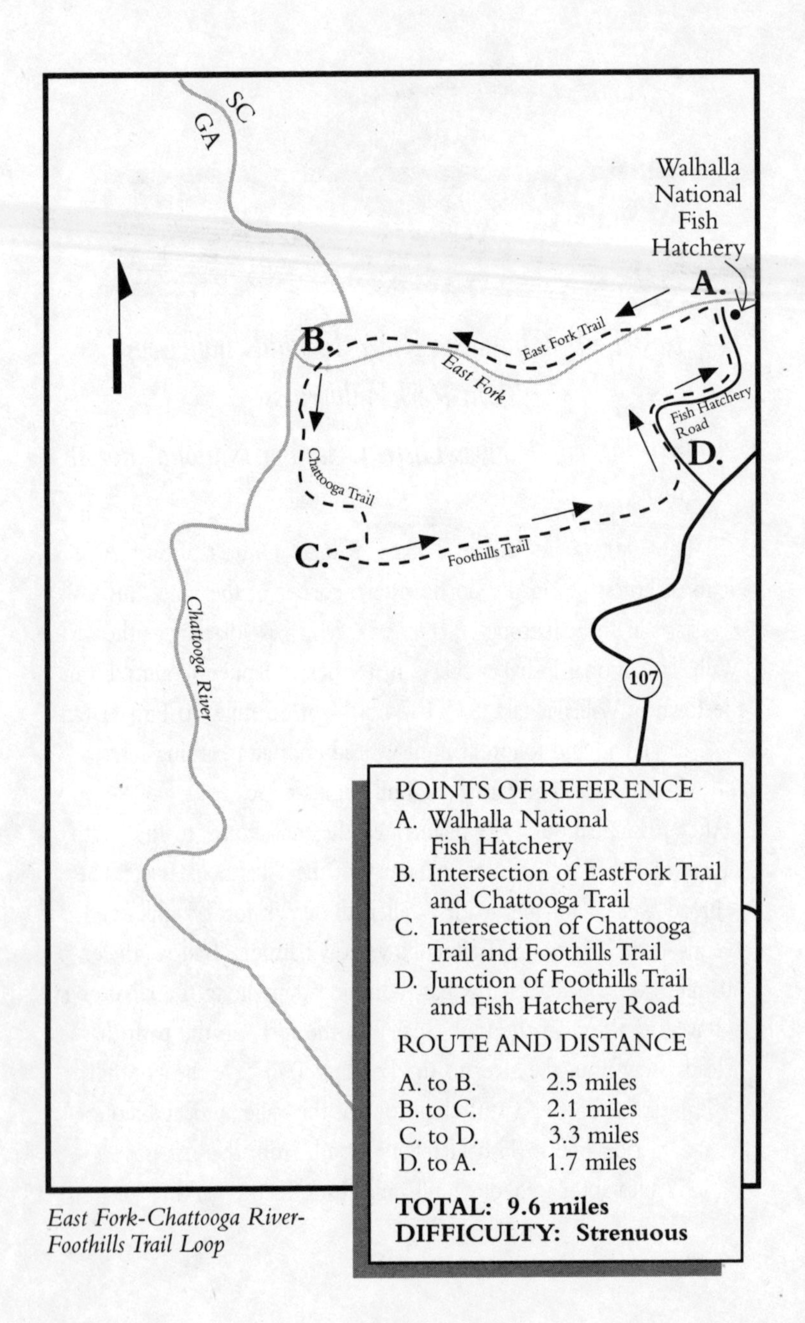

East Fork-Chattooga River-Foothills Trail Loop

Chattooga Country

The Appalachian Mountains occupy only 2 percent of South Carolina's surface area. The line of demarcation between Piedmont and mountains is in the far northwestern corner of the state. North and west of the line is a six-hundred-square-mile sliver of mountainous terrain that has little in common with the rolling hills and flatlands of the rest of the state. The peaks there are not as tall as those in North Carolina or Virginia. The highest, Sassafras Mountain, rises only 3,554 feet, while North Carolina's Mount Mitchell tops out at 6,684 feet. But even with its less-than-spectacular altitudes, South Carolina's mountain province still offers hikers some wonderfully rough country.

Some of the best of it is in Andrew Pickens Ranger District in Sumter National Forest. To the west is Georgia's Chattahoochee National Forest, to the north is North Carolina's Nantahala National Forest, and sprawled across the junction of the three states is the Ellicott Rock Wilderness, a rugged 9,015-acre plat that was designated a wilderness area in 1975. The wilderness is drained by the Chattooga River, which also serves as the boundary line between South Carolina and Georgia.

The Chattooga rises in North Carolina, only ten miles north of the South Carolina border, but it picks up steam quickly, and by the time it reaches the state line it is a substantial stream. It must flow two more miles, however, to its confluence with East Fork, before it becomes a real river. From that point on, the Chattooga is a rampaging bull, dropping over two thousand feet in the next forty miles, until it is tamed by Tugaloo Dam.

Fame came to the Chattooga in 1972, when the movie *Deliverance* was released. Its spectacular wilderness setting and breathtaking white-water canoeing scenes were filmed on the Chattooga, and the river became a cause célèbre for conservationists, who pushed for laws to protect it. In 1974 they succeeded, and the Chattooga was designated the South's first National Wild and Scenic River. The movie also made the river a magnet for seasoned canoeists and rafters—and for a large number of novices. In the three years following the film's release, seventeen people died trying to run the river. Quite a few more came close, including Diane, who took a bad spill at Decapitation Rock in the early 1970s but emerged a hundred yards downstream with her head still attached and only a few bruises. I managed to stay in the raft by attaching myself to the rubberized fabric like a tick to a dog, but the experience left me with a profound respect for the Chattooga and an urge to see it again—on foot.

I arrive at trailhead on an overcast summer morning. The walk I have planned will pass through Ellicott Rock Wilderness and one leg of it will parallel the mighty Chattooga. It begins, however, at the decidedly civilized Walhalla National Fish Hatchery, an operation run by the United States Fish and Wildlife Service. Before heading into the wilderness, I poke around the hatchery. I have had so little success fishing for trout that the idea of seeing a lot of them in one place is irresistible.

The working part of the hatchery consists of twenty-four spotlessly clean concrete tanks called raceways. Each one is a hundred feet long, eight feet wide, and three or four feet deep. Cold water pours into one end of the tanks and drains out the other. I peek into the first raceway, and there they are—hundreds of sleek trout, all facing upstream like soldiers in formation. These are good-sized fish, but they are packed into the tank like sardines in a can. There's not enough room for them to move about much, so they lie quietly, swishing their tails to hold themselves steady in the current, showing only their greenish-brown backs to me.

Hatchery fish are segregated by size, large fish in one tank, medium-sized ones in another, and so on. In the tanks holding the smaller, more playful fish, I can see fingerlings surface and roll, flanks gleaming. The fish in these tanks are so unlike the wary, secretive trout I've encountered that they don't seem of the same breed. But, of course, they are. Many of the trout in South Carolina's rivers and creeks are hatchery raised. And since hatchery-raised trout are far easier to catch than wild trout, it is likely that the few I've hooked grew up right here, in a concrete tank at the Walhalla Fish Hatchery. After wandering around for a few minutes, the assembly-line aspect of the operation begins to bother me, so I hurry out the gate to start my walk.

The trail first passes through a picnic area filled with towering hemlocks and white pines. Although parts of Ellicott Rock Wilderness were logged as late as the 1950s, the trees in the picnic area have been around far longer than that. A guidebook lists the height of one white pine as 165 feet, the tallest in the state. After crossing to the north side of East Fork, the path parallels the creek and passes through a cool, shady area. The vegetation is typical of an Appalachian river forest—ferns and dog hobble, Fraser magnolias and yellow birch, hemlocks and tulip poplars. The trail soon enters a dark tunnel of rhododendron, the most ubiquitous of river-forest trees.

Two species of rhododendron grow wild in the South Carolina mountains. Catawba rhododendron (*Rhododendron catawbiense*) has purple flowers and flourishes on mountain slopes and ridges, but the trees along East Fork are rosebay rhododendron (*Rhododendron maximum*). This species produces lovely clusters of white or pinkish flowers and thrives in the moist soil of the river forest.

The trees are scrawny, brushy things, rarely over twenty feet tall, but like Catawba rhododendron and mountain laurel, they tend to clump together in pure, dense thickets (sometimes called "laurel hells") that would be impenetrable without a trail. Like sourwood, another common tree of the southern Appalachians, *Rhododendron maximum* is a member of the family Ericaceae. But unlike sourwood—whose flowers produce a nectar which bees transform into the tastiest honey in the Appalachians—honey from the rosebay rhododendron, and other types of rhodendron, is poisonous . . . maybe.

Maybe? Isn't the toxicity of rhododendron honey something that ought to be known without reasonable doubt? Yes, it should, but it isn't, at least not to everybody's satisfaction. In the world of natural history—the real and messy and complicated world outside the laboratory—questions like this still exist. Some of them have been around for a long time, too; the story that raised this question, for example, is nearly 2,400 years old:

> The Greeks ascended the mountain and camped in a number of villages which were well stocked with food. There was nothing remarkable about them, except that there were great numbers of bee hives in these parts, and all the soldiers who ate the honey went off their heads and suffered from vomiting and diarrhoea and were unable to stand upright. . . .

The poisoning occurred in 400 B.C. and was described by Xenophon in *Anabasis*, his book about a group of Greek mercenaries who fought their way to the shores of the Black Sea in a region known as Pontus. It is believed that the honey that made the Greeks sick (they all recovered in a day or two) came from bees that had been collecting pollen from the flowers of *Rhododendron ponticum*, a purple rhododendron that was common in the area. Much later, suspected poisonings from rhododendron honey were also reported in England.

It is not clear exactly when or why American naturalists decided that rhododendron honey from eastern North America was toxic, but they did. In his 1948 book on trees, botanist Donald Culross Peattie writes that "The nectar of Big Rhododendron [rosebay rhododendron] makes a distinctly poisonous honey, carefully avoided by the beemasters of the Appalachians." Similarly, the 1980 edition of the *Audubon Society Field Guide to North American Trees, Eastern Region* states unambiguously that "Honey from the rhododendrons is poisonous."

Case closed? Well, not quite. Sue Hubbell, a careful beekeeper and an observant naturalist, gently debunks the poisonous-rhododendron-honey theory in *A Book of Bees* and says that "in this country only mountain laurel gives honey that humans in general should avoid."

Well, is it O.K. to eat rhododendron honey or isn't it? The question led me to Stephen Bambara, an Extension Apiculturist at North Carolina State University. He says that rhododendron's bad reputation may have come from its resemblance to mountain laurel (another member of the Ericaceae family that, as Sue Hubbell noted, is known to produce honey that makes humans sick), a case of guilt by association. But Bambara then cites a book by J. W. Hardin and J. M. Arena, which states that the leaves, twigs, flowers, and pollen of mountain laurel contain andromedotoxin, a substance that is poisonous to humans. And the book states that "Rhododendron and azaleas contain the same toxic principle." Bambara summarizes his position: "I wouldn't recommend eating honey produced by bees that have been collecting from rhododendrons or, for that matter, from any other member of the Ericaceae family." Now, does that finally settle it? Well, not really. Remember that delicious sourwood honey. Sourwood, you may recall, is also a member of the family Ericaceae.

My advice? I have none. But if I ever run into a jar labeled "Rhododendron Honey," I'm going to eat the contents and settle

the question once and for all. I'm no martyr to science, but I don't mind maybe getting sick for a day or two to answer a 2,400-year-old question.

Beyond the rhododendron tunnel, the pleasant gurgle of East Fork gets louder. The trail rises above the stream then descends to its banks, passing a lovely white-water cascade. The air has a light, tangy odor, one I have smelled often in the Appalachian woods. To me, the scent connotes "fresh air," though I have no idea of its source.

Hickories and red maples line the broad path, and a little farther along a log bridge spans East Fork and leads to the south side of the creek. This is the Chattooga Trail, and I follow it south, leaving East Fork behind. For the first time since I started, I am out of earshot of the pleasant, mellifluous sound of rushing water. Gradually, though, another noise imposes itself, a nearly inaudible rumble off to my right. It grows louder, and suddenly the Chattooga is at my feet, a jumble of gray boulders, white-water rapids, and calm blue-green pools. A yellow tent sits beside the river. A man wearing jeans and waders and a tan fishing vest makes his way from the tent to the path. He is a big man, carrying a well-worn fly rod.

We exchange pleasantries. He has yet to catch a fish on this trip, he tells me, so he is going to walk to a special pool he knows beyond Ellicott Rock, a secret pool with wild trout and no people. I consider accompanying him. Ellicott Rock—the rock for which this wilderness area was named—is only a couple of miles upstream, and I would like to see it. I would also like to see his special pool. But I think about the miles I have ahead of me and about the etiquette of following a person to a secret fishing hole, learning its location, and fishing there the next day. I discard the idea; not that I am above such a thing, but he is a big guy and *he* might also be fishing there the next day. I ask him if he's seen Ellicott Rock.

"Sure, plenty of times."

"You've seen the inscription?" I ask, recalling a photograph of the rock that I once saw.

"Yes, but I forget exactly what it says. I think it has some numbers and a date on it. It also says that it marks the North Carolina–South Carolina line."

We talk for a few more minutes, then I wish him good luck, and he strides off, moving upstream, searching for trout. I sit down on the bank of the Chattooga to rest and to reflect on Ellicott and his eponymous rock.

Andrew Ellicott, a well-known surveyor, was hired by Georgia governor D. W. Mitchell to determine the state's northern border. He undertook the project in 1811 and (as nearly as I can tell) finished it in early 1812. In the process, he established the point where South Carolina, North Carolina, and Georgia meet, a spot now known (in most reference books) as Ellicott Rock. The famous inscription carved into the boundary rock reads:

LAT 35
AD 1813
NC + SC

But, like rhododendron honey, nothing in the southern Appalachians is simple. It turns out that the inscription is not Ellicott's. Ellicott's *real* rock is ten feet from the current boundary rock, and it reads (I am told) "1811."

It seems that Ellicott's results were not universally accepted, and in 1813 another team was dispatched to re-survey the border. Ellicott's measurements were found to be slightly off, and it was the new team that chiseled the well-known inscription into the rock. At least one author has picked up on this and refers to the current boundary point as "Commissioners Rock" (see Allen de Hart's *South Carolina Hiking Trails*). But the more precise nomenclature hasn't caught on, and most people, including me, continue to refer to the boulder with the 1813 date on it as "Ellicott Rock."

The Chattooga Trail continues along the river for about a mile, then begins to rise. At a signed junction, I go east on a cut-off trail, moving away from the river toward the Foothills Trail. The galax-lined path crosses a small creek and enters a dark glade of hemlocks. As the trail continues to climb, the land becomes drier, and stands of white pines replace the hemlocks of the moister lowlands. At the next trail junction, I pick up the white-blazed Foothills Trail and follow it east, climbing along a ridge.

Up here, on the dry ridgeline, the trees are mostly maples and hickories, mixed with hollies, sassafras, and loblolly pines. There are even a few chestnut oaks, a species usually found only on the driest slopes in these mountains.

It's nearly mid-morning, and the sun is high and hot. Until now, I have seen and heard very little wildlife: a chickadee or two, crows calling in the distance, a flash of silver near some dimples in the river. But there's plenty of wildlife here along the Foothills Trail. There are spiders surrounded by huge, intricate webs and butterflies of every sort—skippers, sulphurs, swallowtails, and more. There are locusts and huge green grasshoppers and clouds of gnats and midges. In the middle of the trail, I spot a shiny, dark elephant stag beetle, with pincers big enough to twist my foot off if I accidentally stepped on him.

After a mile or so of steady climbing, the Foothills Trail levels off and starts to descend. The walking becomes easier; the forest becomes scrawnier. This part of the trail is outside Ellicott Rock Wilderness, and the area has been logged recently. I pick up my pace and soon reach Fish Hatchery Road, the final, paved, downhill leg.

When I arrive at the parking lot, I have a sense of incompleteness, as if I really haven't finished the walk. So, instead of collapsing on a picnic table as I usually do after a long hike, I head for the hatchery. I stand beside one of the raceways and watch the trout.

The fish—brown, rainbow, and brook trout—are born in the hatchery and kept there for eighteen months, until they are nine inches long. Then they are released into streams and lakes in Georgia, South Carolina, and Tennessee. Although fish are not stocked directly in Ellicott Rock Wilderness, they are added to the streams and rivers nearby that eventually feed into the wilderness. The "wild trout" so eagerly sought by the fisherman I met earlier on the Chattooga are probably fish that came from this hatchery, or their descendants.

This morning I compared the trout in these raceways to sardines in a can, but the longer I watch them, the less accurate that observation seems. The individual fish come and go almost magically, moving up and down, backward and forward in the tank, nudging and hiding beneath one another. I dip a finger into the cold water. The trout scatter like quicksilver. My earlier impression was wrong; these are real trout, all right, not mechanical fish assembled on the production line of a manufacturing plant. They may not be as wary as wild trout, but they are skittish enough to avoid my finger and, I'll bet, any clumsily presented fly I might throw at them. My mistaken notion about the hatchery does not surprise me. The Southern mountains are complex territory, composed of ancient rock layered over even more ancient rock. And nothing about them—not their honey, geography, or trout—is simple.

BEFORE YOU GO

For More Information

Sumter National Forest
Andrew Pickens Ranger District
112 Andrew Pickens Circle
Mountain Rest, S.C. 29664
(803) 638-9568

Accommodations

The nearest lodging is in Walhalla, but the choices are limited to a single motel. For information, contact

Walhalla Chamber of Commerce
220 East Main Street
Walhalla, S.C. 29691
(803) 638-2727

Seneca, seven miles south of Walhalla, offers more options; it has three motels. For information, contact

Greater Seneca Chamber of Commerce
P.O. Box 855
Seneca, S.C. 29679
(803) 882-2097

Campgrounds

There are three developed campgrounds in the Andrew Pickens Ranger District, including one that can accommodate trailers. The Forest Service also provides designated campsites for backpackers. Primitive camping outside the designated areas is allowed, subject to restrictions, in the Ellicott Rock Wilderness and the Chattooga River corridor. For information, contact the Andrew Pickens Ranger District.

Maps

A good map for this walk is "Trail Guide: Andrew Pickens Ranger District, Sumter National Forest." It can be bought for $3.00 at the Forest Service's Stumphouse Ranger Station, just off S.C. 28, or from

U.S. Department of Agriculture
Forest Service
1835 Assembly Street
Columbia, S.C. 29201
(803) 765-5222

Points of Interest

A walk in the Ellicott Rock Wilderness would be incomplete without a visit to the trout tanks at Walhalla National Fish Hatchery. For information, contact

Walhalla National Fish Hatchery
P.O. Box 9
Walhalla, S.C. 29691
(803) 638-2866

Additional Reading

A Book of Bees by Sue Hubbell, Ballantine Books, New York, 1988.

A Book of Honey by Eva Crane, Oxford University Press, Oxford, 1980.

The Chattooga Wild and Scenic River by Brian Boyd, Ferncreek Press, Conyers, Ga., 1990. If you are contemplating rafting, kayaking, or canoeing the Chattooga, this is the book to read. It gives detailed descriptions of what to expect at each of the river's major rapids.

Human Poisoning from Native and Cultivated Plants by James W. Hardin and Jay M. Arena, M.D., Duke University Press, Durham, N.C., 1969.

A Natural History of Trees of Eastern and Central North America by Donald Culross Peattie, Houghton Mifflin Company, Boston, 1948.

The Persian Expedition by Xenephon, translated by Rex Warner, Penguin Books, New York, 1949.

Rhododendron Handbook 1947 edited by N. K. Gould and P. M. Synge, The Royal Horticultural Society, London, 1947.

A CAPTIVATING COVE

Coldspring Branch–Jones Gap–Tom Miller Loop
Caesars Head State Park

The 7,476-acre Caesars Head State Park is 30 miles northwest of Greenville on U.S. 276, not far from the North Carolina border. The walk starts near the Raven Cliff Falls parking area, 1 mile north of park headquarters. The Coldspring Branch Trail begins at a gate just off U.S. 276, 100 yards south of the parking lot.

The well-marked trail starts on a ridge, then follows Coldspring Branch through a lovely cove forest to its confluence with the Middle Saluda River. Just beyond the river, the trail intersects Jones Gap Trail, an old, gently graded toll road that parallels the Middle Saluda River for 2.6 miles to Tom Miller Trail. The Tom Miller then climbs the last 0.8 mile back to Raven Cliff Falls parking area.

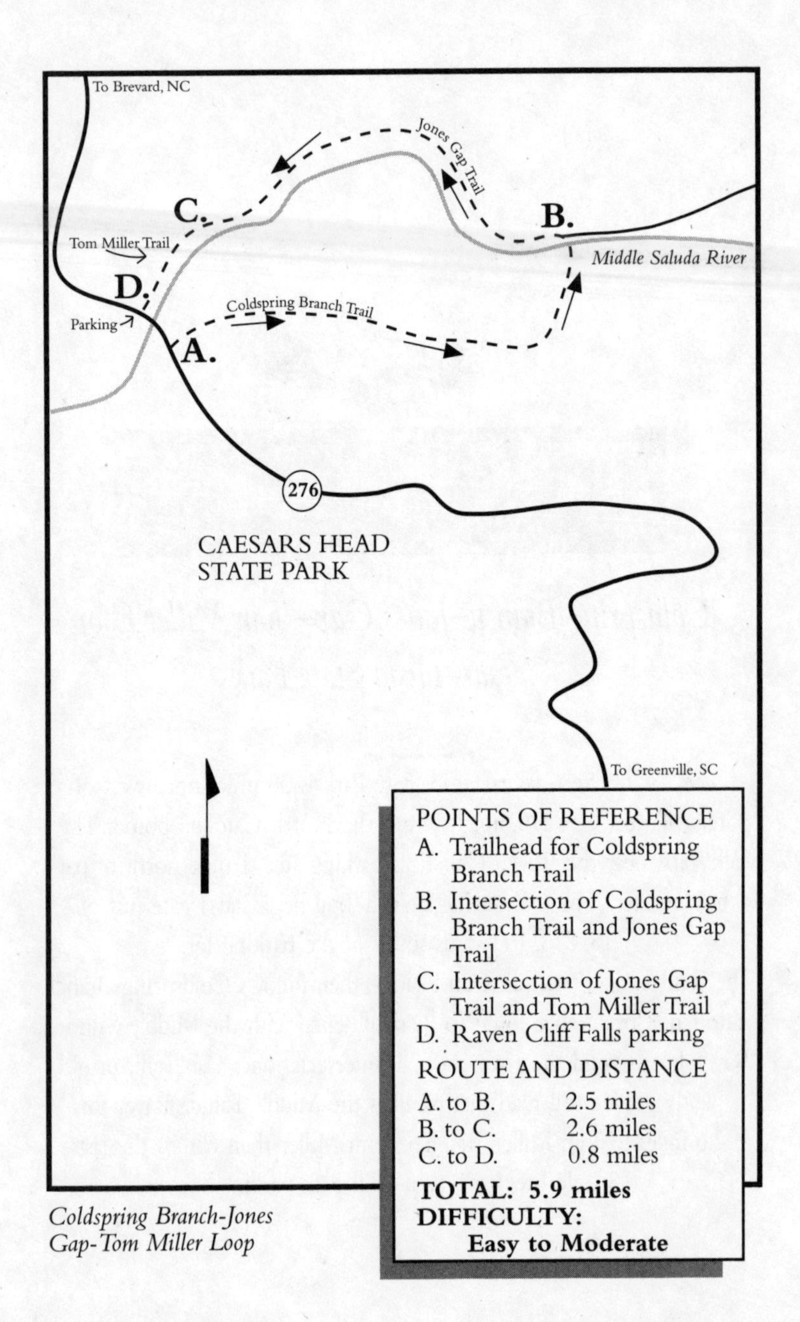

Coldspring Branch-Jones Gap-Tom Miller Loop

A Captivating Cove

The great scarp called Caesars Head rises abruptly from the rolling hills of the Piedmont to an altitude of 3,266 feet. When viewed from a certain angle, the granite outcropping is said to resemble the profile of a head. The head, however, has no chin, so the resemblance is vague—as is its connection to Caesar. Prior to becoming a state park in 1979, Caesars Head was privately owned, and tourists were charged a fee to take in the views from the top of the scarp. It is possible that some early owners of the property decided on the name "Caesars Head" rather than

"Bubba's Head" or "dramatic, but ugly, rock outcropping" for reasons that had more to do with marketing than any similarity to the dead Roman.

Today, the headquarters of Caesars Head State Park sits atop the escarpment, and the views are free. The park, along with the adjacent Jones Gap State Park, and land administered by the South Carolina Department of Wildlife and Marine Resources make up the twelve-thousand-acre Mountain Bridge Wilderness and Recreation Area. Excellent trails crisscross the wilderness area, but the Coldspring Branch–Jones Gap–Tom Miller loop is special. It passes through one of the most appealing landscapes in the upcountry, a lovely mountain cove.

My dictionary defines a *cove* as "a small sheltered inlet or bay" or "a deep recess or small valley in the side of a mountain: a level area sheltered by hills or mountains." The two definitions appear to be unrelated, referring in one case to a body of water and in the other to a mountain valley. In fact, both types of coves have something important in common: they are sheltered areas, protected from the elements, places of refuge.

In the southern Appalachians, coves are enclosed by ridges that shield them from the strong, desiccating winds that rake the mountains in winter. Since the Appalachians get a lot of rainfall, the absence of drying winds in the coves makes them damp places, with numerous branches and streams coursing down the interior flanks of the surrounding ridges to the river valleys that drain them. The moisture moderates temperatures in the coves, cooling them in summer, warming them in winter. In early summer, the result is a cool, dark pocket of lush vegetation and diverse wildlife—the perfect place for a long walk on a warm day.

I start the orange-blazed Coldspring Branch Trail on a fine June morning. It is hot and overcast in the lowlands but cool and clear in the mountains. Ten steps from trailhead and I am enclosed by forest. The rumble of traffic is replaced by the twittering of robins, the rustle of leaves. There are activities as enjoyable as walking on a broad path through an Appalachian forest in the early morning—but not many.

The trail descends through a medley of sizable trees: yellow buckeye, northern red oak, beech, sugar maple, tulip poplar, and Fraser magnolia. Half an hour later, I hear the first murmurings of Coldspring Branch. The ground, the air, and the dew-covered vegetation become wetter as the trail follows the creek deeper into the cove. Hemlock and small white pines appear in the forest, and Fraser magnolias become larger and more numerous. It's shady and cool down here, and ferns carpet the ground beside the trail. A two-inch-long, bright-orange, stubby-legged creature crawls out of the green understory onto the path and pauses, allowing me a good look. It is a subadult eastern newt (*Notophthalmus viridescens*), also known as a red eft—a stage in one of the more complicated life cycles to evolve on the planet.

Newts superficially resemble lizards; they are small four-legged creatures with long tails. But lizards are reptiles, and newts, like their cousins the frogs and toads and salamanders, are amphibians. Their skin is permeable to water, and they have no claws, scales, or ears. Within the Class Amphibia, the newts fall into the Order Caudata, or tailed amphibians, which in North America consists of seven families. Perhaps to confuse laymen, scientists have assigned names like "Ambystomidae" and "Plethodontidae" to the salamander families, while the newts are found in the family Salamandridae. Except for skin texture (salamanders are slimy; newts aren't), some salamanders closely resemble the newts, and unless you are a herpetologist or a skin stroker, it is often hard to tell one from the other.

Like salamanders, newts start their lives in water. In spring, the fertilized eggs of the eastern newt hatch into greenish-yellow larvae with short legs, keeled tails, gills, and tiny teeth. Though they are less than a half-inch long, these critters—like their parents—are carnivorous. During the summer they swim about in whatever puddle or stream they were born in, eating anything smaller than themselves. Come fall, some subspecies of the eastern newt, including the red-spotted newt found in these mountains, undergo an adolescent transformation, a startling change in appearance and behavior that makes the onset of acne and bad manners in our own species seem minor. They turn bright orange, lose their gills, and leave the water for the forest floor. They become, in a word, efts.

I kneel beside the one on the path. He seems harmless and a little sluggish, but I am not fooled. Like adolescents of most species, efts are voracious feeders, consuming prodigious numbers of springtails and other small insects. But it is merely a phase; after one to three years, an eft's skin darkens to a brownish olive-green, and it takes to the water again and becomes a proper adult newt, feeding and reproducing and carping about rebellious orange-skinned teenagers.

The trail continues to descend, crisscrossing Coldspring Branch. Dog hobble grows beside the path, and moisture-loving river birches flourish near the stream. At the bottom of the trail is the Middle Saluda River, a torrent of clear, cold water tumbling along a boulder-strewn stream bed. The Middle Saluda was the first river to be designated as a Wild and Scenic River by the state of South Carolina. And from where I stand, looking upstream, perched precariously on the narrow log that serves as a bridge across the river, the honor seems appropriate. Moments later, while standing knee-deep in the river, after falling from the narrow log that serves as a bridge across it, I am even surer. Down here, the cold, rushing waters are downright breathtaking. So I stand in the middle of the stream for a few minutes, cursing and gasping for air, while South Carolina's first Wild and Scenic River tugs at my jeans, soaks my boots, and chills my feet.

Just beyond the Middle Saluda, Coldspring Branch Trail intersects Jones Gap Trail, and I begin the easy climb out of the cove. There are beeches and hemlock and hickories along the path, but the most common tree is the Fraser magnolia. Down here, in the heart of the cove, these magnolias seem very happy. In fact, somewhere among all the other magnolias in this cove is the state-record Fraser magnolia.

The Fraser magnolia (*Magnolia fraseri*) is a favorite of mine. I admire its huge cream-colored flowers and the clumps of large leaves that spread from the tips of its branches like dark-green parasols. I also appreciate the telltale lobes at the base of those leaves which differentiate the Fraser from all other local magnolias, making it impossible to misidentify. This feature must have been important to others as well, since another common name for the species is the ear-leaved umbrella tree.

The species is named for John Fraser (1750-1811), an enterprising Scottish nurseryman who, according to one source, "took more American plants to English gardens than any other person," but the first botanist to describe the tree was William Bartram. Bartram, a fearless traveler, set off on horseback from Charleston for the "Cherokee nation" on April 22, 1776. Later, in western South Carolina, probably not far from here, he stopped and studied the tree that would later be named the Fraser magnolia. He had noticed them before "particularly on the high ridges betwixt Sinica and Keowe," but here, he said, on "the highest ridge of the Cherokee mountains . . . it flourishes and commands our attention." Bartram was so impressed with the trees he saw there that he named the spot "mount Magnolia."

The trail continues its gentle climb, passing yellow buckeyes and eastern hemlocks, basswood and hickories. Beneath the trees are mountain laurel and dark rhododendron. Ferns and wildflowers border the hard, narrow track, and the walking is fast and easy.

After leaving Jones Gap Trail for the Tom Miller Trail, though, the path begins to rise steeply, and I soon stop to rest. All day long I have heard birds rustling about and singing in the trees, but I have yet to see one clearly and I haven't recognized any of their songs. As I sit quietly by the trail, one finally holds still in the top of a hemlock long enough for me to get my binoculars on it. A tiny bird with a yellow head, black breast, and white stripes on its wings peers nervously down at me. It is a black-throated green warbler (*Dendroica virens*). According to my field guide, it is one of the more common eastern warblers, with a distinctive voice that makes it easy to identify—at least for Roger Tory Peterson.

These birds nest from the southern Appalachians to Canada, but being sensible creatures, they winter in south Florida or Mexico or Central America. Warblers amaze me, and the black-throated green is no exception. That these five-inch birds manage to migrate a thousand or more miles every year is remarkable. The hazards they must survive on those flights—storms and predators and simple navigational errors—seem overwhelming.

Understandably, the ones that do make it to South Carolina, are wary, twitchy creatures that will sit still only for a moment before vanishing into the forest's green canopy—as does the one I am watching.

As the path climbs to the top of the ridge, the ground and foliage become drier. By the time I reach the parking lot at the end of the trail, oaks and hickories, along with a smattering of dogwoods and tulip poplars, prevail. Of course, the tree that once dominated this mountain forest—the American chestnut—is long gone, the victim of a blight imported from Asia. For the chestnut, the protection of a mountain cove proved to be more illusion than fact. And today, the very idea of what "protected" means, at least from an ecological point of view, is beginning to be questioned.

The efts and frogs and salamanders of Caesars Head State Park, for example, were once thought to be protected by the laws of the state and by the mountains that enclose this cove. But the amphibians of the park are under attack today as surely as the chestnuts ever were.

Throughout the world, amphibian populations are collapsing. Since no one actually knows what the world-wide population of amphibians is today, or was ten years ago, the evidence is anecdotal. The issue surfaced in 1989, at the first World Congress of Herpetology. Many of the scientists attending the conference reported that amphibians were harder to find than usual, and when they did find them, there were fewer of them. Surprisingly, the villain wasn't just the usual habitat destruction; amphibians were disappearing from the pristine, protected areas of the world, as well as from those where the land had been disturbed.

The golden toad of Costa Rica's Monteverde Cloud Forest Reserve is suddenly near extinction, and the gastric brooding frog of Australia is gone. In Britain, the crested newt is declining, and the once-plentiful Cascades frog of the Pacific Northwest has become increasingly rare. What's going on here? is a question herpetologists hear frequently. And, like most groups that are confronted with hard questions and scarce data, the answers given by its members vary considerably. Taken together, they amount to "Round up the usual suspects."

The usual suspects in this case range from "extreme [population] fluctuations [that] might be chronic among . . . some amphibians" (in other words, there is no problem) to a signal of worldwide "environmental stress" (code for the natural world's coming to an end, soon). Between these extremes, the causes given for amphibian decline sound like the familiar litany of environmental problems: acid rain, high concentrations of pesticides and other pollutants in soil and water, increased ultraviolet radiation because of damage to the ozone layer, and global warming. They all make sense. The amphibians' permeable skin probably does make them vulnerable to acid rain and other poisons; their lack of fur or feathers or scales might indeed sensitize them to an increase in ultraviolet radiation; and their cold-bloodedness would certainly make them susceptible to global temperature changes—just as the dinosaurs were. (Or might have been; some scientists now believe that dinosaurs were warm-blooded.)

These days, we seem to be getting hit regularly with widespread ecological problems like this one, problems that transcend local, man-made boundaries. The spruce-fir forests of the southern Appalachians mountains are dying, as are the spruces of the Black Forest in Germany. Songbirds—including many species of warblers like the black-throated green—are declining throughout North America, and some, like Bachman's warbler, once common in some areas of South Carolina, are presumed extinct. The dogwoods of the east coast—like the chestnuts before them—are suddenly vulnerable to a fungus of unknown origin.

As with the dwindling amphibian population, these problems, and their root causes, are not local but are continent-wide or even planet-wide in scope. Thus, little can be done at a single location—even in the most sheltered mountain cove—to protect the species affected. When it comes to pests and pollution, the cliché "global village" is truly applicable. The days of protecting a species by simply tightening a state law or shutting down a nearby source of pollution—though those things can help—are long over. Like the problems themselves, real protection now demands global action.

In the case of amphibians, the scientific community is divided between those who want to do something now—anything!—and those who believe that more data are needed. When you are not sure of the dimensions of a problem—or even if one really exists—solutions come hard. I can add little to this brouhaha, except to echo the sentiment Rachel Carson expressed in *Silent Spring*, her 1962 classic on the dangers of pesticides. "Future generations are unlikely," Carson wrote, "to condone our lack of prudent concern for the integrity of the natural world that supports all life." Amen.

BEFORE YOU GO

For More Information

Caesars Head State Park
8155 Geer Highway
Cleveland, S.C. 29635
(803) 836-6115

Accommodations

The closest lodging is in Brevard, North Carolina. For information, contact

Brevard Chamber of Commerce
35 West Main Street
Brevard, N.C. 28712
(704) 883-3700

Campgrounds

There are no developed campgrounds in Caesars Head State Park or in the Mountain Bridge Wilderness and Recreation Area, but camping is permitted, after registering with a ranger, at seventeen primitive sites along the Jones Gap Trail. The nearest public campgrounds are in Table Rock State Park. For information, contact

Table Rock State Park
246 Table Rock State Park Road
Pickens, S.C. 29671
(803) 878-9813

Maps

The trails are well marked, and the map on the back of the free park brochure, "Mountain Bridge Wilderness Hiking Trail Map & Camping Information" is suitable for this walk.

Additional Reading

"Caesar's Huff" by Dan Harmon, *Sandlapper* 1, January/February 1990, 25-28.

"Frog in the Night-time: The strange case of the vanishing amphibians" by David Quammen, *Outside* XVIII, May 1993, 39-48.

"A Good Frog is Hard to Find" by Beth Livermore, *Smithsonian* 23, October 1992, 113-120.

Handbook of Salamanders by Sherman C. Bishop, Hafner Publishing Company, New York, 1962. This edition is a reprint of a 1947 book published by Cornell University Press.

A Short History of Botany in the United States edited by Joseph Ewan, Hafner Publishing Company, New York, 1969.

Silent Spring by Rachel Carson, Houghton Mifflin Company, Boston, 1962.

Travels of William Bartram by William Bartram, edited by Mark Van Doren, Dover Publications, New York, 1955. This book was originally published in Philadelphia in 1791 under the title *Travels Through North & South Carolina, Georgia, East & West Florida,*

The Cherokee Country, The Extensive Territories of the Muscogulges, Or Creek Confederacy, And The Country Of The Chactaws.

Where Have All the Birds Gone? Essays on the Biology and Conservation of Birds That Migrate to the American Tropics by John Terborgh, Princeton University Press, Princeton, New Jersey, 1989.

A HEALING FOREST

Oconee and Old Waterwheel Trails
Oconee State Park

Oconee State Park's 1,165 acres lie 12 miles northwest of Walhalla on S.C. 107. The Oconee Trail starts in the park, across the street from the parking lot for the carpet golf course. The trail starts west, then proceeds south and east around a sizable lake. At an intersection 2.0 miles from trailhead, the Oconee Trail continues left, while the orange-blazed Old Waterwheel Trail goes right. The latter descends to a creek; the original site of the waterwheel is a few hundred feet to the right. The Old Waterwheel Trail continues left, curling north and west until it rejoins the Oconee Trail. From there, it is 0.1 mile to the Foothills Trail and only a few hundred yards farther to a paved road. The final mile of the loop is on this lightly traveled park road.

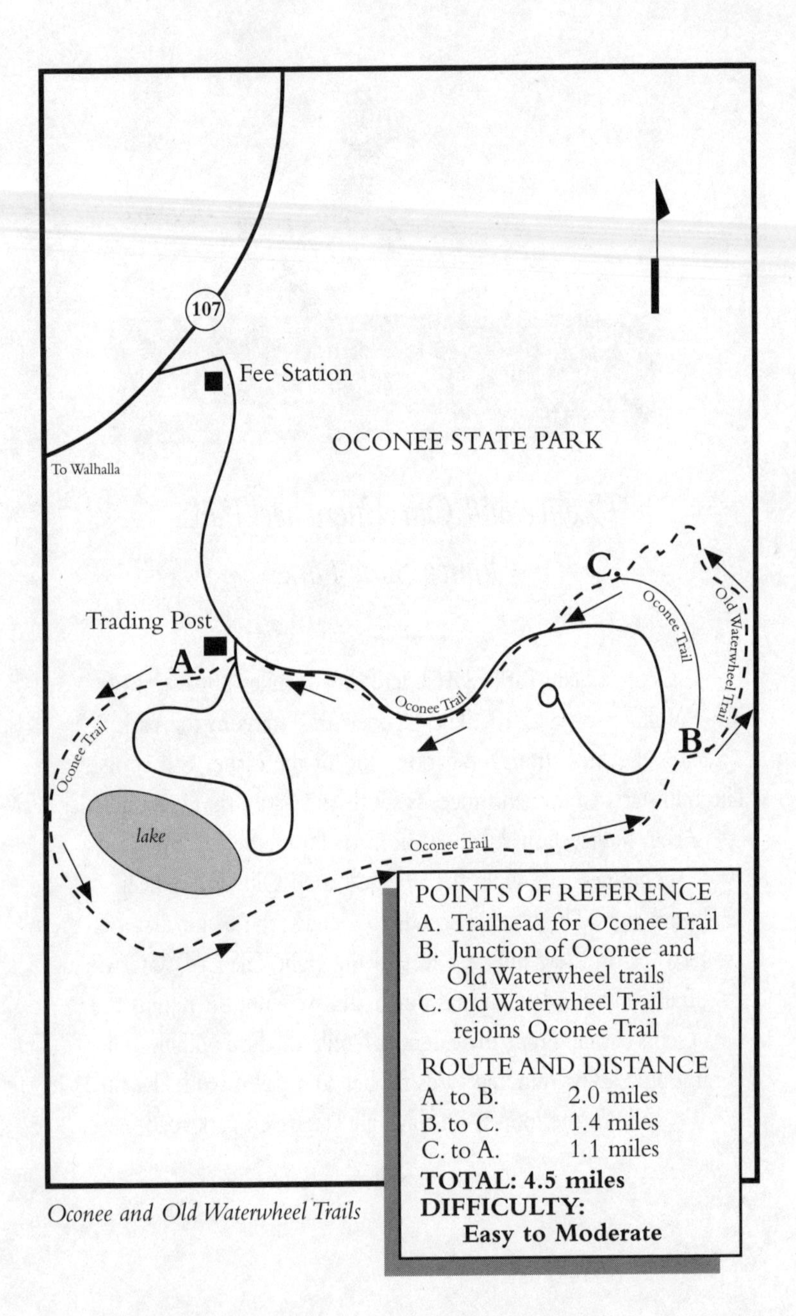

Oconee and Old Waterwheel Trails

A Healing Forest

From Edisto Beach to Parris Mountain, the buildings and fences and picnic shelters of South Carolina's older state parks have a distinctive, rustic look. Because these structures were built from stone and logs and rough-cut lumber, taken from nearby sites or from the parks themselves, they fit their natural surroundings perfectly. But that doesn't explain the numinous aura about them. That comes from the painstaking craftsmanship that went into their construction—the perfect fit of the hand-notched braces of a picnic shelter or the harmony of stones in a low-slung fence. The result is structures of such uniformly high quality that they appear to have been assembled by a single, inspired hand.

The first park I ever visited was one of those older parks. Like many other Columbians, my first brush with the outdoors took place at Sesquicentennial State Park. I was young then, and impressionable, so I was imprinted with that characteristic look, the look that says, "This place is a park."

"The look" is not confined to South Carolina parks. Parts of Rocky Mountain, Yosemite, and Big Bend national parks were also written on by the same hand. So were the Blue Ridge Parkway, Sumter National Forest, and many other natural areas. Obviously, the hand was not—could not have been—that of a single individual, no matter how inspired. It was, instead, the work of a single, inspired organization, known to its members as the "Cees" and to the rest of us as the Civilian Conservation Corps, or the CCC.

The CCC was established by congress under the Emergency Work Act. President Franklin Roosevelt proposed the legislation on March 27, 1933. The bill, less than two pages long in its final form, passed both houses of congress and was back on Roosevelt's desk for his signature within four days. Three months later, 275,000 men were at work at 1,300 CCC camps across the country, and by 1935, the legislation had created jobs for 600,000 men in 2,650 camps. One of the camps, F-1, was on 1,165 acres of eroded, farmed-out mountain land donated to the state by Oconee County in 1925. On it, the youths of the CCC dammed a stream to create a 20-acre lake and built picnic shelters, vacation cabins, and hiking trails. The result was Oconee State Park, a park that looks today very different from the way it must have looked when it opened in 1937. The shelters and cabins and stone fences built by the CCC still stand, pretty much unchanged.

The lake and spillway also must look about the same. But the beat-up, farmed-out land—the park's setting in the 1930s—has changed dramatically. Nobody knows how many of the 58,266,696 trees that the CCC planted in South Carolina were set out here, nor how many of them are still standing, but the mixed, second-growth pine-and-hardwood forest that covers the park has the same sense of belonging here that the CCC-built structures do. The best way to get a sense of the forest created by Roosevelt's two pages is by walking the Oconee and Old Waterwheel trails. They can be combined into a 4.5-mile loop that explores this rejuvenated land, a part of the CCC's legacy to the state that is even more important than picnic shelters and rock walls.

I start the Oconee Trail on a cool, overcast day in late fall. The leaf season peaked about a week ago, but yellows and reds still cling stubbornly to the maples and hickories along the trail. Virginia pines, American hollies, and an occasional white pine add splashes of green to the colors of the hardwoods. The path is brown with oak leaves that crunch satisfyingly under my boots, while the herbaceous layer is thick with switch cane, a knee-high grass found throughout the South.

The trail arcs southwesterly around a lake. My presence annoys a small flock of mallards, which quack loudly and swim away from shore. A lovely, purplish-blue wildflower blooms beside the path. I squat beside it, field guide in hand.

The plant is easy to identify; only a few wildflowers are in bloom this time of year. It is, the book tells me, a soapwort gentian (*Gentiana saponaria*), a rare perennial. The colorful two-inch-long flowers sit atop an undistinguished plant with dull-green, lance-shaped leaves. The plant itself is almost completely hidden by switch cane, and I would have surely missed it had it not been in flower. The showiest wildflowers often come from the smallest, drabbest plants, which proves, I suppose, that modest beginnings—like Roosevelt's two pages of legislation—sometimes do produce extraordinary results.

Beyond the lake, the trail passes through a grove of white pines. Their fine, brown needles mat the forest floor and soften the path. White pines are valuable timber trees, often the first in the forest to fall to the logger's axe, so it is likely that these were planted by the CCC after the land was protected. And though they would be dwarfed by the 150-foot-tall white pines that were once common in the virgin forests of the Northeast, they are still substantial trees, and it's nice to see a reminder of that great boreal forest here in the South.

Beyond the pine grove, the trail enters a dark thicket of mountain laurel, then climbs into a hardwood forest of oaks and maples and fiery red sourwoods. Dog hobble, galax, and runty sassafras trees grow beside the path. A large, gray hornets' nest, deserted and forlorn at this time of year, hangs from a small hickory, and a gray squirrel scampers through the branches of a nearby white oak. The stiff, green leaves of a Fraser

magnolia have turned yellow and droop like a collapsed umbrella; it has given up on fall and, like the hornets, is waiting for winter.

The most plentiful trees on the dry slopes of this ridge are oaks, mostly white oaks, Southern red oaks, and chestnut oaks. The leaves of these trees often change directly from green to brown in the fall and rarely produce intense colors. However, these woods are brighter than most oak forests. The reason is the presence of scarlet oaks, trees whose fall colors rival those of the maple and sourwood.

The scarlet oak (*Quercus coccinea*) is not uncommon in the mountains and inner Piedmont of South Carolina, but it is unusual to see so many in one spot. I examine several trees and soon find what I am looking for. A gall—a brown, papery sphere about the size of a crab apple—is hidden in the oak's brilliant red foliage. Galls occur on many (perhaps all) species of oaks, but this particular one, the oak apple gall, is most often found on *Q. coccinea*.

Galls fascinate me. For a time my fascination took the form of merely wondering what they were and what caused them. But as I learned more, my interest deepened. I found out that galls are local swellings of plant tissue caused by infections. The source of infection can be almost anything, from fungi, viruses, and mites to insects and nematodes. Beyond that, however, not a lot is known about galls. Even oak apple galls, one of the larger and more common types of galls, are one of the least studied phenomena in the forest. One reason for this is that few people have ever seen the critters that cause them.

Oak apple galls are the egg chambers of wasps of the family Cynipidae. Cynipid wasps are glossy black or brown insects with short, thick abdomens and hunched shoulders. Unlike the social hornets that built the nest I saw earlier, cynipid wasps are solitary creatures. They are also tiny, which is why many naturalists overlook them. The smallest insect known, the oddly named *Alaptus magnanimus*, is a cynipid-like wasp less than one-hundredth of an inch long. The wasps responsible for oak apple galls are bigger, but they are still less than a quarter inch in length.

The females of most (but not all) cynipid wasps lay their eggs in plants. Each species specializes in a particular variety of plant or tree. For example, the California oak gall wasp lays its eggs in California white or black oaks, while the live oak gall wasp specializes in the California live oak. The oak apple gall of the East is caused by an insect with an even odder name than *A. magnanimus*. The culprit is *Amphibolips confluenta*, a cynipid wasp whose best-known feature is the gall it produces on the twigs of oaks.

For years, naturalists thought oak apple galls were caused by a chemical secreted by female wasps when they deposited their eggs in the living tissues of a tree. But scientists later found out that the gall does not begin to form until after the eggs have hatched. So, it is the larvae themselves that cause galling. Precisely what chemicals these larvae give off is not known, though, nor is the chemical composition of the gall itself. All we know is that some chemical or chemicals produced by the larvae react with the tree's tissues and cause swelling (or galling), and that the swollen tissues then become food for the immature wasps. The gall I am looking at has a hole in it where the larvae inside chewed an exit. (The larvae make the exit holes before pupating into wasps.) The hole is not much larger than a pinprick. How could specks of life small enough to get through this tiny hole create a gall so much bigger than themselves? No one knows the answer, but the question is worth considering, if only for what it tells us about the state of the natural sciences today. In an age when genetically engineered plants are becoming as common as pine trees, galls and gall-makers are perfect examples of how little we really know about the natural world. As the renowned scientist and essayist Lewis Thomas put it, "The only solid piece of scientific truth about which I feel totally confident is that we are profoundly ignorant about nature. Indeed, I regard this as the major discovery of the past hundred years of biology."

Not far beyond the scarlet oaks, the trail descends into a hollow filled with large white oaks. The air is sweet smelling and crisp, and the browns of winter mute the bright colors of fall. I think I can see the healing hand of the CCC in this forest. I don't know if they planted trees here or sandbagged erosion gullies or cleared away brush to check the forest fires so common in their day, but this land is healthy and about as far from farmed-out as you can get.

After passing through more hollows and climbing more ridges, the Oconee Trail intersects the Old Waterwheel Trail, which then begins a steep descent to a creek. At the creek, the trail forks. I take the path to the right, toward the site of the old waterwheel.

The creek is fast-moving and clear, but narrow, no more than ten feet across. It flows through a shallow gorge, made lush by profusions of rhododendron, Christmas ferns, and dog hobble. Only a few hundred feet from the trail fork stands an old, moss-covered stone house, the original site of the waterwheel installed by the CCC to pump water from the creek up to their camp. Stone pillars, which once supported a wooden raceway that carried the water to turn the wheel, stand gray and solitary in an unruly tangle of dark-green rhododendron.

After exploring the site, I backtrack from the wheelhouse and follow the Old Waterwheel Trail upstream. Near some large beech trees, I hear a startlingly loud *doodlee, doodlee, doodlee*. I find a log, sit down, and try to spot the bird that is singing. I know what to

look for; this is one bird call I always recognize. In fact, I hear it, or some variation of it, almost every day from a brush pile outside my office window. I see him regularly, too, so I know the species well. My resident singer is a loudmouth Carolina wren, the state bird of South Carolina.

The Carolina wren (*Thryothorus ludovicianus*) is a permanent resident of the state and is found throughout it, from the lowest swamps to the highest mountains, from the wildest woods to the tamest suburbs. The wren I am listening to is typical of the species. It flits about in the underbrush, occasionally letting loose with its boisterous three-part song. It moves so quickly and so erratically that it is hard to locate, but it finally tires of the game and hops up on a log not more than thirty feet from me. It is a perky looking bird, about the size of a sparrow, with a warm reddish-brown body, a defiant upturned tail, and rakish white stripes over its eyes.

Carolina wrens will nest almost anywhere, from brush piles to mailboxes. In *South Carolina Bird Life*, Sprunt and Chamberlain write about one that nested in a mayonnaise jar on a back porch. But to me the most amazing thing about these birds is their loudness. These tiny wrens have very big voices. The one outside my window is so noisy that it often forces me to stop work and just listen for a while. My wife has even suggested that I'd rather listen to the wren than work. She may have a point. I manage to find a reason every year not to clean up our brush pile, and I'm thinking about setting out a mayonnaise jar.

The last leg of the walk starts with a stiff climb away from the creek. The path then rejoins the Oconee Trail, which ends at a paved park road that takes me back to the parking lot.

From there, I wander over to an exhibit behind the bathhouse where the original CCC waterwheel is displayed. Signs explain how the overshot wheel drove a ram pump which moved water nearly a mile from the creek up to the CCC camp. A second sign explains how the arrival of electricity in the Oconee area in 1941 made both wheel and pump obsolete. There is a wistfulness about the signs and exhibits, a feeling that the old days were the good days, despite the hardships endured by those who lived through them.

A third sign stands near the entrance to the park office. It tells of the depression years in South Carolina, about the hard times, and about Franklin Roosevelt and the fine work of the fifty-thousand men that worked in the state's CCC camps. This sign, too, has a nostalgic quality about it, as if the author would like to see it all happen again: first, a few bad years, then two pages of miracle-producing legislation.

In fact, some people have suggested that a new organization similar to the CCC might benefit the country. Such an organization, they argue, would create decent outdoor jobs for disadvantaged youths, who would use their muscle and enthusiasm to heal the land. It's a good idea, but Oconee won't need them. The trees, planted and nurtured by the young men of the original CCC, are maturing into a healthy, glowing forest, harboring wasps and wrens, wildflowers and tall scarlet oaks. And after nearly sixty years of use, the picnic shelters and cabins they built are holding up well. No, Oconee doesn't need another Civilian Conservation Corps. The first one did the job just fine.

BEFORE YOU GO

For More Information

Oconee State Park
624 State Park Road
Mountain Rest, S.C. 29664
(803) 638-5353

Accommodations

The state owns and operates nineteen heated and air-conditioned vacation cabins in the park. They are furnished with linens, pots and pans, and eating utensils. For reservations, contact the park office.

Campgrounds

A 140-site camping area with heated restrooms and showers is tucked away in the hardwood forest south of the park office. Reservations are not accepted for campsites. A primitive campground is available for groups.

Maps

Both trails are well blazed, and the free map provided by the park, although not drawn to scale, is adequate for this walk.

Fees

Entrance to the park is free except on summer weekends, when a $2.00 parking fee is charged.

Points of Interest

The museum attached to the park office has an exhibit, "Trout Fishing in the Southern Appalachians." There is also a collection of old tools, many of which were used by Civilian Conservation Corps employees in their daily lives and in their construction projects. There are wooden washing machines, churns, and crosscut saws. There are wooden wheel barrows, wagon wheels, acetylene torches, and much more. The tools are well worn, but like most things the CCC touched, they are still in generally good condition.

Additional Reading

Biology of Gall Insects by T. N. Ananthakrishnan, Edward Arnold (Publishers) Ltd., London, 1984.

Biology of Insect-Induced Galls edited by Joseph D. Shorthouse and Odette Rohfritsch, Oxford University Press, New York, 1992.

Eastern Forest Insects by Whiteford L. Baker, U.S. Department of Agriculture, Forest Service Miscellaneous Publication No. 1175, Washington, 1972.

"Field Trip: Oconee State Park" by Greg Lucas, *South Carolina Wildlife* 40, September/October 1993, 52-55. The author, accompanied by two experienced naturalists, walks the Old Waterwheel Trail.

A Guide to Familiar American Insects by Herbert S. Zim and Clarence Cottam, Golden Press, New York, 1987. This little field guide has good nontechnical drawings of the interior and exterior of an oak apple gall.

"Heritage of Hard Times" by Glenn Oeland, *South Carolina Wildlife* 39, July/August 1992, 16-29.

Plant Galls and Gall Inducers by Dr. Jean Meyer, Gebruder Borntraeger, Berlin, 1987. Translated by S. Cheskin.

Roosevelt's Forest Army: A History of the Civilian Conservation Corps 1933–1942 by Perry H. Merrill, published by the author, Montpelier, Vt., 1981.

South Carolina Bird Life by Alexander Sprunt, Jr., and E. Burnham Chamberlain, University of South Carolina Press, Columbia, 1949.

Wildflowers of North Carolina by William S. Justice and C. Ritchie Bell, The University of North Carolina Press, Chapel Hill, 1968.

The World of the Wasp by Joy O. I. Spoczynska, Crane, Russak & Company, Inc., New York, 1975.

Acknowledgments

I am grateful to Diane Manning, who illustrated the book, edited each chapter, and accompanied me on many of the walks. Without her, there would be no *Palmetto Journal*.

The Monday Night Writers' Group—Dorrie Casey, Susan Ballenger, John Manuel, Mary Russell Roberson, and Maura Stokes—made their usual constructive suggestions and kept me on the trail when I tried to wander.

Authors often trade book-publishing stories. If there is a better organization for a writer to work with than John F. Blair, neither I nor my acquaintances have run into it. Carolyn Sakowski and her staff know the publishing business well, and it is a pleasure to watch them convert a raw, typewritten manuscript into a book.

Each chapter in the book has its own bibliography, but they do not include some of the references that I used almost every day—some in the office and others on the trail. Without them, my own book would have been less accurate and, I suspect, less enjoyable.

Audubon Society Field Guides

I own almost every one of these little gems. They have proved useful on the trail and off. Their thumbnail sketches of natural history often provided the starting points I needed to dig further into the lives of the plants and animals I found on my walks.

The Roger Tory Peterson Field Guide Series

Like most birders in the eastern United States, I rely on Peterson's *Field Guide to the Birds East of the Rockies* when I am afield. Another guide in the series, *Eastern Trees*, was also useful.

Finding Birds in South Carolina by Robin M. Carter, University of South Carolina Press, Columbia, 1993.

This book was helpful because of its detailed directions to many of South Carolina's natural areas. It is also an excellent guide to finding birds in the state.

South Carolina Trails, Second Edition, by Allen de Hart, The Globe Pequot Press, Chester, Connecticut, 1989.

This book lists most of the trails in the state. It provided the starting point for many of the walks in this book, and I often used it to help determine the mileages for those walks.

South Carolina Wildlife

I have issues of this magazine going back to the 1960s, and they were the first place I looked for information on South Carolina's natural areas.

When I finish a walk, I like to spend time with the people who run our parks and refuges and national forests, the men and women who manage the land and develop and maintain the trails; the folks who band ducks, plant trees, and deal with the public. They are the heroes and heroines of this book, and it is their hard work that makes it possible for the rest of us to enjoy South Carolina's natural areas.

Somehow, in addition to their normal duties, these people also found the time to answer my questions about titi and cherrybark oaks, about cynipid wasps and red-spotted newts, spruce pines and cotton rats. Many of them vetted chapters, and their comments helped me weed out inaccuracies. So, my special thanks go to Layne Hamilton, refuge manager, Pinckney Island National Wildlife Refuge; Pat Metz, wildlife interpretive specialist, Savannah Coastal Refuges; Mike Caulder, ranger, Huntington Beach State Park; Keith Windham, superintendent, Huntington Beach State Park; Mike Foley, chief resource manager, South Carolina Department of Parks, Recreation & Tourism; Gurden Tarbox, president, Brookgreen Gardens; Pete Range, biologist and master birder, Cape Romain National Wildlife Refuge; George Garris, superintendent, Cape Romain National Wildlife Refuge; Mike Spivey, superintendent, Edisto Beach State Park; Mike Dawson, assistant sanctuary manager and patient explainer of the hydrology of Four Holes Swamp, Francis Beidler Forest; Fran Rametta, park naturalist, Congaree Swamp National Monument; Robert S. McDaniel, superintendent, Congaree Swamp National Monument; Tommy Strange, waterfowl manager and tough-minded reader, Santee Coastal Reserve; Gail Fuller, administrative assistant, Santee Coastal Reserve; Bill Mason, assistant refuge manager and brackish-water-marsh authority, Santee Coastal Reserve; Kim Hofeldt, ranger, critic, and fellow mosquito hater, Witherbee

Ranger District, Francis Marion National Forest; Ricky Ingram, refuge manager of Carolina Sandhills National Wildlife Refuge, one of the better-run wildlife refuges I've ever visited; Larry Williams, assistant refuge manager and dog lover, Carolina Sandhills National Wildlife Refuge; Dave Robinson, forester, Carolina Sandhills National Wildlife Refuge; Kay McCutcheon, office manager, Carolina Sandhills National Wildlife Refuge; Mack Copeland, superintendent, Keowee-Toxaway State Park; Joel Gardner, acting district ranger, Edgefield Ranger District, Sumter National Forest, and district ranger, Long Cane Ranger District, Sumter National Forest (While I was writing this book, Joel's responsibilities were expanded, and he was put in charge of both the Edgefield and Long Cane ranger districts. When he received a second manuscript to vet, he didn't cry foul but sat down and produced another fine job.); Marty Kindred, assistant ranger, Long Cane Ranger District, Sumter National Forest; Don Seriff, park naturalist and eft expert, Mountain Bridge Wilderness Area; Tammy Sutherland, seasonal naturalist, Caesars Head State Park; Horace Jarrett, district ranger, Andrew Pickens Ranger District, Sumter National Forest; Greg Borgen, ranger, Andrew Pickens Ranger District, Sumter National Forest; Stephen Bambara, extension apiculturist, North Carolina State University; Andy Davis, superintendent, Oconee State Park; and Ken Ahlstrom, an entomologist at the North Carolina Department of Agriculture, who taught me something about cynipid wasps and oak apple galls and other buggy topics.

Finally, though many people helped in the preparation of this book, I alone am responsible for any omissions and errors that remain.

Index